Witches of Plymouth County
And Other New England Sorceries

Compiled and Edited

by

Edward Lodi

Rock Village Publishing
41 Walnut Street
Middleborough MA 02346
(508) 946-4738

Witches of Plymouth County
And Other New England Sorceries

Compiled and Edited

by

Edward Lodi

ROCK VILLAGE PUBLISHING
MIDDLEBOROUGH, MASSACHUSETTS
First Printing

Witches of Plymouth County
Copyright © 2004 by Edward Lodi

Typography and cover by Ruth Brown

ISBN 0-9721389-4-3

Dedication

To Yolanda,

who was born on Halloween
and who has bewitched me these many years

Contents

Introduction

There are three categories of witches: white ones befriend man and help him in any way possible; grey ones use magic for their own purposes but are not actively good or bad; while black witches compact with the Devil to bring evil into all things. — J.A. *Brooks,* Ghosts and Witches of the Cotswolds

Mention Salem, Massachusetts, and the word *witch* immediately comes to mind—rightly so, given that town's infamous seventeenth-century trials and executions. Mention Plymouth, however, and sentimental images of straitlaced Pilgrims and Plymouth Rock and the first Thanksgiving are more likely evoked. But like Salem early Plymouth had its witches, both real and imagined. The fact that none were hanged, burned at the stake, or pressed to death, though creditable, does not fully exonerate our Pilgrim forefathers from the sins of bigotry.

In Plymouth Colony the practice of witchcraft—along with sundry other nasty crimes such as treason, murder, and buggery— was punishable by death. Though infrequently, innocent people were indeed arrested and brought to trial. In 1661 Goodwife Holmes of Marshfield was accused of being a witch. Fortunately her accuser, nineteen-year-old Dinah Sylvester, who claimed that she saw Holmes change herself into a bear, was not believed, and she herself stood trial for, and was found guilty of, defamation and had to pay a fine.

In 1677 Mary Ingham of Scituate was indicted for having, through witchcraft and with the help of the devil, brought harm to the body of Mehitable Woodworth, causing her "to fall into violent fitts...causing great paine unto severall parts of her body att severall times, soe as shee, the said Mehitable Woodworth, hath been almost bereaved of her sencis." Fortunately for Mary the authorities came to their "sencis" and she was acquitted of all charges. But we can imagine the extent of her suffering and mental anguish, knowing full well that if found guilty she would forthwith, and without mercy, be put to death.

Later, in the eighteenth century, Plymouth witches of notoriety such as Moll Ellis, Aunt Rachel, and Mother Crewe—if we accept as fact the folk tales recounting their sorcerous misdeeds, the spells and curses that caused ships to sink and their neighbors to sicken and die—probably should have stood trial and faced the death penalty for their crimes. But of course in our enlightened age we don't accept such fantasies as fact.

Do we?

Witches, real and imagined...

This is not so much a book about the history of witchcraft as it is a book about how witches were once perceived in Plymouth County and in other localities within Massachusetts and throughout New England. It is a book of folklore as well as of fact. It is also, to some extent, a personal history. No, I am not now nor have I ever been a witch. But I knew one, many years ago. Perhaps I should refer to Monteej as a *warlock*, since he was a he and not a she. But as a child, ignorant of the niceties of language, I thought of him as a *witch*—and old habits are hard to break. Or, taking my cue from Charles M. Skinner (writing of one "John, or Edward, Dimond") should I simply refer to him as "a benevolent wizard?"

As a writer of ghost stories I am repeatedly asked: *Are these stories true?* It is a question I cannot always answer with precision. Wherein lies truth? And the same equivocal "answer" holds "true" for many of the stories included in this book. Obviously some are folk tales, in their day fervidly believed by narrators and listeners alike, but no longer given credence, not even by the most naive among us. A couple are admittedly pure fiction and are labeled as such. Then there is the matter of Monteej—and the baroque and fervent imaginations of a pair of gullible young children. What *really* happened in the remote woods of Plymouth County on that fateful September night more than a half century ago?

Along with the more fanciful tales I've included a smattering of historical fact (to demonstrate just how widespread, how prevalent and deeply ingrained, was the belief by our ancestors in witchcraft), as well as some purely (and perhaps wildly) speculative notions (such as the role, however minor, that alcoholism might have played in the belief in, and persecution of, witches in colonial New England), notions which more serious scholars might want to consider, even if they eventually dismiss them, as being, uh, just a little farfetched.

Finally, what business you may ask do I have mixing history with folklore? Are not the two mutually exclusive? Does not the former have to do with witnesses and documents and recorded fact? And the latter with fantasy and superstition and imagination?

Valid questions, to which I posit still another (albeit a rhetorical one): what is more fantastical than the actual (i.e., historical) testimony—accepted as unassailable by the courts— of the "witnesses" and "victims" in the notorious Salem witch trials? For example (selected more or less at random): "She and Martha Carrier did both ride on a stick or pole when they went to the witch meeting at Salem Village, and that the stick broke as they were carried in the air above the tops of the trees, and they fell. But she did hang fast about the neck of Goody Carrier and were presently at the village, that she was then much hurt of her leg." Such testimony resulted in the hanging of nineteen men and women and the imprisonment of scores of others.

Or consider this (from "A Sketch of the Life of Nathaniel Hawthorne," published in 1896 as an introduction to *The Whole*

History of Grandfather's Chair): "One of Hawthorne's own ancestors had been a judge who had condemned innocent people to death because he believed them guilty of witchcraft. A visitor to Salem court house is shown now a bottle containing some large coarse pins, such as were made a couple of hundred years ago, and is told that these pins were found sticking into children's bodies, and some old woman was accused of being a witch and sticking them in, though no one saw her do it. It seems foolish enough to us who look at the old bottle of pins today, and hear the steam trains and electric cars go whizzing by outside, but it was a very serious matter in the Salem of witchcraft times."

With the subject of witchcraft it is sometimes impossible to separate fact from fiction, history from folklore. Take for instance the matter of the Wilbur Witches (included in the "Bewitched, Bothered, and Bewildered" chapter in this book). This folk tale seems to have had its origins in the actual haunting of the Wilbur family by a poltergeist (similar to the Bell Witch in Tennessee). But eventually it grew into a more traditional witch story with suspicion being cast upon an old woman, Granny Bates, of among other things taking on the shape of a cat.

In the end if these stories (true, imagined, or otherwise) entertain, and to some extent inform— as to the customs, superstitions, and lifestyles of our Yankee forebears—well, let that suffice.◊

witches of plymouth county

In West Barnstable a Mr. Wood charged Liza Tower Hill with putting a bridle and saddle on him and riding him many times to Plum Pudding Pond in Plymouth, where witches held nightly orgies. —Amos Otis, Genealogical Notes of Barnstable Families, *as noted in* Jonathan Draws the Long Bow *by Richard M. Dorson*

Aunt Rachel's Curse

...the possibility that enchantment lay behind the destruction of vessels lost at sea did not escape settlers...A common belief in the bay area held that a powerful witch could sink ships without a trace by placing a saucer in a pail of water. The container was shaken vigorously, and when the saucer overturned the vessel would capsize and sink to the ocean floor. —Sally Smith Booth, The Witches of Early America

(from *Myths & Legends of Our Own Land* by Charles M. Skinner, 1896)

On a headland near Plymouth lived "Aunt Rachel," a reputed seer, who made a scant livelihood by forecasting the future for such seagoing people as had crossed her palm. The crew of a certain brig came to see her on the day before sailing, and she reproached one of the lads for keeping bad company.

"Avast, there, granny," interrupted another, who took the chiding to himself. "None of your slack, or I'll put a stopper on your gab."

The old woman sprang erect. Leveling her skinny finger at the man, she screamed, "Moon cursers! You have set false beacons and wrecked ships for plunder. It was your fathers and mothers who decoyed a brig to these sands and left me childless and a widow. He who rides the pale horse be your guide, and you be of the number who follow him!"

That night old Rachel's house was burned, and she barely escaped with her life, but when it was time for the brig to sail she took her place among the townsfolk who were to see it off.

The owner of the brig tried to console her for the loss of the house. "I need it no longer," she answered, "for the narrow house will soon be mine, and you wretches cannot burn that. But you! Who will console you for the loss of your brig?"

"My brig is stanch. She has already passed the worst shoal in the bay."

"But she carries a curse. She cannot swim long."

As each successive rock and bar was passed the old woman leaned forward, her hand shaking, her gray locks flying, her eyes starting, her lips mumbling maledictions, "like an evil spirit, chiding forth the storms as ministers of vengeance." The last shoal was passed, the merchant sighed with relief at seeing the vessel now safely on her course, when the woman uttered a harsh cry, and raised her hand as if to command silence until something happened that she evidently expected.

For this the onlookers had not long to wait: the brig halted and trembled—her sails shook in the wind, her crew were seen trying to free the cutter—then she careened and sank until only her mast-heads stood out of the water. Most of the company ran for boats and lines, and few saw Rachel pitch forward on the earth—dead, with a fierce smile of exultation on her face. The rescuers came back with all the crew, save one—the man who had challenged the old woman and revengefully burned her cabin. Rachel's body was buried where her house had stood, and the rock—before unknown—where the brig had broken long bore the name of Rachel's Curse.

Notes

Aunt Rachel's use of the term "moon cursers" in her denunciation of the man who threatened her may require an explanation. In *It's an Old Cape Cod Custom* Edwin Valentine Mitchell devotes a chapter to the subject and writes: "Wild stories used to be told of the wreckers of the Cape, who decoyed ships ashore by the use of false lights. Mooncussers they were called, because the moon interfered with their business, and they cursed it." For an even fuller account of the practice, see Henry C. Kittredge's *Mooncussers of Cape Cod.*

Not surprisingly, Cape Cod is the locale of another tale of a witch's malison upon a ship.

Marillis Bittinger includes "The Curse of Old Mother Melt" in *Tall Tales of Cape Cod.* "Old Mother Melt lived in an ancient, ragged cottage on the outskirts of Provincetown." Like many a lonely old woman, she was looked askance upon by the townsfolk, who—seeking a scapegoat to account for their ills— tended to blame her for any untoward event. "The threat that 'Old Mother Melt will get you' disciplined many an obstreperous child."

Despite her unsavory reputation, Captain Samuel Collins, about to set sail on a whaling voyage, agreed as a favor to take on her fifteen-year-old son as cabin boy and apprentice. Because of some mix-up or mishap, the boy did not show up in time and the ship sailed without him. As it left the harbor, however, "Mother Melt was at the wharf shrieking a curse upon the ship and all its hands."

The inevitable occurred. A powerful storm arose from nowhere, washed several crewmen overboard, and caused the ship considerable damage, forcing it to limp back into Truro. Understandably upset, Captain Collins set off to kill Mother Melt, but her pleas stayed his hand, and with her promise "to never again utter a curse," he spared her life. Not only that, but he took on her son as apprentice. Eventually, the boy became master of his own ship and "enjoyed a remarkable record of clear sailing," presumably under his mother's good auspices.◊

Mother Crewe

From witches and wizards, and long-tailed buzzards,
And things that run along hedge-bottoms,
Good Lord, deliver us! —an ancient prayer

(from *Myths & Legends of Our Own Land* by Charles M. Skinner, 1896)

Mother Crewe was of evil repute in Plymouth in the last century. It was said that she had taken pay for luring a girl into her old farm-house, where a man lay dead of small-pox, with intent to harm her beauty; she was accused of blighting land and driving ships ashore with spells; in brief, she was called a witch, and people, even those who affected to ignore the craft of wizardry, were content to keep away from her.

When the Revolution ended, Southward Howland demanded Dame Crewe's house and acre, claiming under law of entail, though primogeniture had been little enforced in America, where there was room and to spare for all. But Howland was stubborn and the woman's house had good situation, so one day he rode to her door and summoned her with a tip of his whip.

"What do you here on my land?" said he.

"I live on land that is my own. I cleared it, built my house here, and no other has claim to it."

"Then I lay claim. The place is mine. I shall tear your cabin down on Friday."

"On Friday they'll dig your grave on Burying Hill. I see the shadow closing round you. You draw it with every breath. Quick! Home and make your peace!" The hag's withered face was touched with spots of red and her eyes glared in their sunken sockets.

"Bandy no witch words with me, woman. On Friday I will return." And he swung himself into his saddle.

As he did so a black cat leaped on Mother Crewe's shoulder and stood there, squalling. The woman listened to its cries as if they were words. Her look of hate deepened. Raising her hand, she cried, "Your day is near its end. Repent!"

"Bah! You have heard what I have said. If on Friday you are not elsewhere, I'll tear the timbers down and bury you in the ruins."

"Enough!" cried the woman, her form straightening, her voice grown shrill. "My curse is on you and hereafter. Die! Then go down to hell!"

As she said this the cat leaped from her shoulder to the flank of the horse, spitting and clawing, and the frightened steed set off at a furious pace. As he disappeared in the scrub oaks his master was seen trying to stop him. The evening closed in with fog and chill, and before the light waned a man faring homeward came upon the corpse of Southward Howland stretched along the ground.

Although Charles M. Skinner believed Mother Crewe to be little more than a fanciful figure from folklore, another author—of greater talent and more lasting fame—knew her for what she was, an actual historical personage.

Jane Goodwin Austin (1831-1894) wrote a number of popular books based on early American history, most notably *Dr. LeBaron and His Daughters*, a rather lengthy (460 pages of small print) yet highly readable novel about colonial Plymouth and some of the surrounding towns that make up Plymouth County. In the book she brings alive, through scenes both dramatic and domestic, the period from roughly 1740 until shortly after the American Revolution. Though the novel centers around Dr. LeBaron and his numerous progeny, Mother Crewe appears throughout, as both a main character and a unifying force—albeit *unifying* only in a thematic sense; in the dramatic sense she is the exact opposite, that is to say, a destructive force. Regardless, Austin leaves no doubt in the reader's mind that Mother Crewe existed in fact as well as in folklore. As she wrote in her preface, "A Word of Explanation:"

I t is with some hesitation that I offer to the public this story of Doctor LeBaron, including as it does so many other of the Old Colony chronicles; and this, for the trite old reason that truth is stranger than fiction, and therefore more incredible. It is these incredible truths, however, that give its color to the folklore of any given epoch, and every student of our country's early history has discovered that our forefathers lived as intensely, if not as scientifically, as we do. They had, to be sure, no railway accidents, steamboat explosions, or "tramp-wire" catastrophes, but they supped full of horrors in the way of witchcraft, cursing, demoniacal possession, murder, lawless love, and broken hearts; in fact, found in their own surroundings all that vital stimulus which we are apt to count as outgrowth of our advanced civilization.

The story of Mother Crewe's curse, with its results, is substantially true, and the scene depicted in chapter xliv [concerning Southward Howland, in part reprinted below] is literally so...In fact, there is no memorable incident related in these pages that is not matter either of history or well-founded tradition in the Old Colony, and though our modern taste may revolt at the crude coloring and realistic limning of these pictures of the past, we must piously preserve them as the shadows of those who, being dead, yet speak, and that in the language of their day rather than ours.

"The story of Mother Crewe's curse" begins when her beloved daughter, Bathsheba, who is betrothed to the fickle Ansel Ring, falls seriously ill. Mother Crewe hires a young lass, Molly Peach, to help care for the ailing girl. Unfortunately, and perhaps predictably, Molly and Ansel fall in love even while poor Bathsheba lies on her death bed. More culpably, Molly contrives, with Ansel's reluctant assistance, to withhold from Bathsheba medicine which Dr. LeBaron has provided for her, thereby hastening her death.

Mother Crewe discovers their treachery, and acts accordingly:

"Mother Crewe!" gasped Molly, her face blanching piteously. "Yes, Bathsheba Crewe's mother!" shrieked the old woman. "Bathsheba, that you murdered, you two—yes, murdered—the only child I had, and she lying in her grave and you dancing on it; but not for long, mark you, not for long, if a widow's curse can hender."

"Oh, don't curse us, don't curse us!" screamed Molly, falling on her knees and covering her face with her hands.

But Mother Crewe's face showed no sign of relenting as she

gazed upon that trembling figure, decked out with its poor attempt at bridal finery; indeed, an added scorn and detestation seemed to gather upon her brow, and bending over the girl, her arms stiffly extended upward, she deliberately cursed her in all the detail of anathema to be gathered from the black and bitter pages of wizard lore: sleeping, waking, in her home and among her neighbors, in her body and in her soul, in her life and in her death, and in a dishonored grave. "And may your husband fail in all he undertakes and die of a broken heart, and may all your sons be cripples, and all your girls lightlied and deserted as mine has been, and no one to pity or to help."

[It's not long before the effects of the curse are felt.]

In a wretched hovel upon the Carver road lived and died the family of Ansel Ring and his wife Molly, consisting, besides the parents, of three girls with one brother older, and one, poor Ichabod, younger than themselves. Ansel, not much daunted at first by Mother Crewe's curse, had pursued his seafaring life, and as he was a strong, sober, and able-bodied seaman had no trouble in getting employment from one or other of the firms of shipping-merchants of Plymouth, then carrying on an active commerce with all parts of the world.

But his fellow-sailors were also many of his fellow-townsmen, and all the world knows how the pressure of immensity upon a sailor's mind generally results in superstition, so that one scarcely wonders that, after two or three fatal mishaps upon the vessels rating Ansel Ring as A1 seaman, some of the other Plymouth men muttered the story of the curse to those who had not heard it, and others spoke menacingly of Jonahs who should be heaved overboard; and the mates, gathering the cause of moody looks and dark hints, carried them to the captains, who laughed grimly and swore contemptuously at such notions, but next voyage did not accept Ring's somewhat hang-dog offer of his services.

The upshot of all this is that Ansel, despairing, commits a rash act that is really an act of suicide, and thus ends his misery. His offspring fare no better. "Poor Ichabod," his youngest child, is crippled at the age of seven by a runaway horse, only to linger painfully for months before finally succumbing to his injuries. And it is the loving and trusting Yetmercy, Molly and Ansel's daughter, whom Mother Crewe treacherously lures into the cabin wherein a man lies dead of smallpox, so that the young woman contracts the disease and dies a horrible death.

Nor can the oldest son, also named Ansel, escape the curse. From childhood he has been deeply devoted to Hannah Howland, but dares not profess his love lest she likewise fall victim. Eventually he dies at sea, frozen to death during a terrible winter storm.

It is Hannah's brother, Southward, who with such dire and fatal consequences lays claim to the land near the Carver road on which Mother Crewe's "dilapidated and squalid cabin" stands. After the episode (presented above in Skinner's version, but dramatized much more vividly and at far greater length in Austin's book) a "day of terror occurs." The sky turns strangely yellow.

Darkness had now fully fallen—a darkness so intense that it seemed ponderous and palpable rather than the mere absence of light—a darkness through which struggled no light of moon or stars, but into whose intensity was woven strange gleams of phosphorescence from the sea, whose waters broke in lines of glowing fire upon the beach, while out of its gleaming distances came ever and anon that strange murmur, those moans and sighs and vague melodies, that the old sailor had recognized as the song of sirens. As the actual night drew in, the darkness deepened in more than the usual ratio of night to day, so that the obscurity which, in the hours of daylight, had been fearful because it was like night, became, so soon as it was night, yet more fearful because it was like nothing ever experienced before by those who endured it.

The Day of Judgment has come! was the cry of those who believed, and non-believers no longer scoffed at such possibilities, but gazed upon each other with bewildered and anguished doubt.

[In the confusion a small boy becomes lost in the woods. He is found the next day in the cemetery, on Bathsheba's grave— having been saved and comforted by none other than Mother Crewe, in whose dead arms he lies cradled. So, partially at least, she has redeemed the evil she brought about with her curse.

The boy's grateful mother says to the men who helped search for the child:] "She fed him, and sung him to sleep in her arms. Men, bury her in her daughter's grave for the sake of your own mothers and of this dear child whose life she saved."

So spoke the woman, and was obeyed, so that in her death Mother Crewe was more honored than in her life.◊

Rochester's Witch Rock

Let me hasten to make it clear that I have no leaning whatever in an occult direction. Nor have I any inside knowledge of, or desire to enter into any magical or necromantic practice. Nothing could distress me more than to open a letter which I had imagined would contain an invitation to a cocktail party, and discover that on account of my writing I had been credited with a spurious evocation of such dark arts and was pressed to join the local coven!—Dorothy Jacob, Cures and Curses

In colonial America every town, it seems, had at least one person who claimed to be a witch—or who, even though making no such claim, was yet feared by others as being in league with the devil. The venerable Plymouth County town of Rochester was no exception. As late as 1934, Alice Austin Ryder wrote in *Lands of Sippican* of one such person: "'Oh, Yes! there were witches in the Center when I was a girl! Ann Cook! She would come to the door and ask for food, and nobody dared to refuse her!' So says a relative of the good captain Cole who gave his life for his crew.

"'If you refused, she would say, 'You'll be sorry by and by!' and sure enough some thing would be bound to happen.

Everybody was scared of her.'

'Why, one day Father and I were driving over to New Bedford, and she stopped us on the road and Father says, 'Go long with you,' and she shook her fist at him, and sure enough before we had gone very far a wheel came off, and we had a dreadful time!'

'Oh Yes! There were witches in Rochester!'"

Ironically, one of Rochester's earliest prominent citizens came to reside in the town as a result of witchcraft. It happened this way:

(from *Old Rochester and Her Daughter Towns*, by Mary Hall Leonard)

Rochester was settled shortly before the fearful period of agitation in the northern towns of Massachusetts over the subject of witchcraft. In 1692, Mark Haskell of Salem, being drawn as a juror in one of the witchcraft cases and deeming them unjust and illegal, declared (so the story goes) that he would get away as far from Salem as a horse could carry him in twenty-four hours. At midnight preceding the trial he packed his saddle bags and rode from Salem to Boston and thence to Rochester, where his numerous descendants may be found today. No important traditions of witchcraft are known to belong to old Rochester, though one vine-covered romantic-looking boulder about a mile from the Center is known far and near as the "Witch Rock."

By a strange coincidence (or not so strange, the subject of this book being witchcraft) two of those "numerous descendants" of Mark Haskell are featured in "Old Colony Witch Stories" by William Root Bliss, reprinted in the next chapter in this book.

The "Witch Rock" that Leonard mentions was so called, not for any associations it may have had with actual witches, but because of a belief by the Indians that devils came from its crevices. Up until roughly the mid nineteenth century, any phenomenon that was perceived to be of supernatural origin would have been spoken of in terms of bewitching. The Bell Witch, in Tennessee, is perhaps the most famous example of this: it was more a poltergeist than anything else; certainly not a "witch" in the ordinary sense.

Devils notwithstanding, Witch Rock has painted on it, in black, the profile of a stereotypical witch. I remember, in the 1950's, being fascinated by the old gal. I lived in the neighboring town of Wareham. Whenever my parents took the "back roads" through Rochester to New Bedford we would pass Witch Rock; they would always slow down so that I could get a good look.

What is it about large rocks that so fascinates? Consider the following:

(from *Mattapoiseett and Old Rochester* by Mary Hall Leonard)

In Central Rochester...there are several interesting rocks, among which may be named Witch Rock, on the corner beside the "Old Country Road." Further back in the woods is "Indian Pound Corn," a large table rock formation showing the indentation made by the Red Man's pestle. There is also a "Devil's Rock," which, like many other similar rocks of New England, shows the definite impress of the foot of the imp as he leaped from the boulder, although this particular Devil's Rock bears an added confirmation of its genuiness, in that William Harris, Sr., actually saw the fiend when he took the final leap.

I've visited "Indian Pound Corn" on several occasions (it's located in woods near an ancient esker, on private property)

and sitting on its flat surface have placed my hand in the indentation where, over a period of hundreds, perhaps thousands, of years, countless kernels of corn were methodically pounded into meal. Did I only imagine, or did I actually feel, faint vibrations, as if the spirits of long-dead Indians were still pounding away?

As for "Devil's Rock," I haven't seen it. Presumably it's not the Devil's Rock which Professor Delabarre of Brown University mentions in his book, *Dighton Rock*. That Devil's Rock was first described by Dr. Ezra Stiles (in the June 7, 1768, entry in his journal): "Rock 1½ m NW from Acushnet—Writing—near Moses Washburn—K Philip." Delabarre writes: "What the connection was between King Philip and the Writing Rock [Stiles] does not state. Mr. Louis W. Tilden of New Bedford has kindly investigated this reference for me. He located the Moses Washburn farm and talked with Mr. Skiff, its present owner." Mr. Skiff was aged 86 at the time, Tilden reported, "'but has a good memory. He knows of no rocks with inscriptions about there, but does recollect a huge boulder called Devil's Rock, which bore a so-called impression of a human foot...This rock was demolished back in the forties to supply stone for the New Bedford City Hall.'"

On November First—the day after Halloween—I gave a talk in Middleborough on the subject of hauntings in southeastern Massachusetts to an audience of approximately sixty-five women. (It would be gratifying to report that the women had gathered for the sole purpose of hearing my presentation, but alas, not so. They were members of a women's club who held regular monthly meetings; I just happened to be that month's guest speaker. My audience was, per force, a captive one.)

I mention this because of what happened after the talk: one

of those mind-boggling coincidences that make writing about the paranormal an exciting adventure rather than an onerous chore.

I had spent several hours that morning working on the first part of this chapter—recording what I knew of Witch Rock, and wondering how I could learn more about its history, in particular, who first painted the witch, and why. After the talk, which ended around one o'clock, I lingered with my wife in the hall where the meeting had been held, chatting with members of the audience and signing books. As I was about to leave for home a woman approached. "Are you familiar with Witch Rock, in Rochester?" she asked.

"Yes," I replied, somewhat taken aback. "Funny you should mention it. I'm currently working on a book about witches and I've been doing research on Witch Rock—though without much luck, I'm afraid."

"I grew up in the house on the property where the rock is located. It was my step-mother who painted the witch."

My wife and I exchanged glances. A chill ran up and down my spine. (That cold shiver: it's a cliché but it happens! Quite often, in fact, when your subject is ghosts and the supernatural.)

"You know," the woman said, "when I found out you were going to talk about ghosts I almost got up and left. But I'm so glad I stayed."

Needless to say, so am I! The remainder of this chapter comprises, for the most part, information she provided.

Joan Thompson (her married name is Maciel) was only four and a half years old when her family moved into the house on the corner of Vaughan Hill Road and New Bedford Road. That was around 1945. Her father, a widower with five children, had just remarried. At that time the house lacked electricity and running water. Joan recalls the two-seater outhouse out back, as well as a cow, sheds, and horses and a wagon. Without question, Rochester in those days was decidedly rural.

As the family grew—to a total of ten children—Drescott Thompson added rooms to the house and made a number of other improvements. One "improvement" to the property which he didn't count on, however, was the painting—of a witch (peaked hat and all) astride a broom, with the words "Witch Rock, Rochester" underneath—that appeared one day on the rock.

Witch Rock, Rochester

One of the Thompsons' neighbors was a librarian; another was the librarian's daughter. It was they who told Shirley (Mrs. Thompson) of the rock's reputation. "There are books in the library that mention Witch Rock and the history behind it. Your house is called Witch Rock Cottage."

A talented artist, Shirley Thompson—inspired by all the stories and legends surrounding the rock—took it upon herself one day to paint on it the profile of the flying witch and the identifying words. (Later, she hand-painted the witch on plates, which she sold to townspeople and summer visitors. I'd like to get my hands on one of those!)

"When my father came home and saw the painting on the rock he was quite upset," Joan remembers. "I thought he'd have a heart attack."

Handpainted Witch Rock Plate

Evidently with time he became reconciled to his wife's art work; a photograph from a local newspaper, taken years later, shows him proudly posing by the rock beneath the witch's flight path.

Witch Rock remains a landmark in Southeastern Massachusetts—the ancient mystery surrounding it lives on, tweaking the imaginations of new generations—largely because Shirley Thompson took the legend seriously and utilized her creative talent to give it pictorial representation.◊

Old Colony Witch Stories

(from *The Old Colony Town and the Ambit of Buzzards Bay* by William Root Bliss)

Many a New England village has had its witch, its haunted house, its graveyard ghost, and its goblin stories. Its children have been afraid to go to bed in the dark, and are afraid now, lest "the Boogers" catch them. These mysterious creatures are supposed to haunt the darkness of bed-chambers and to live by day in some obscure cubby-hole in the garret.

There are two women, descended from one of the English settlers of the Plymouth colony, who tell witch stories and believe in the existence of witches, or of old women who can exercise a supernatural power over others. Their mother and grandmother, for they are sisters, held to the same superstition. In their day a belief in the working of evil influences was almost universal with the lower classes of people in the county, and witchwood was gathered under peculiar circumstances to be kept as a shield against the witcheries of mumbling and wrinkled hags.

Farmers were then particular to cut their cordwood "on the decrease of the moon;" a death in the family was told to the bees, and sometimes the hives were trimmed with crepe, as if it were possible for the wandering spirit of the dead to come back to the homestead to get a supply of honey, if stinted of it in the last resting-place. Akin to this superstition was a custom prevalent in some English colonies of burying a suicide in the cross-roads and driving a stake through the body, to prevent the spirit from coming back to vex the community.

"After you pass Carver Green on the old road from the bay to Plymouth," said one of these women, "you will see a green hollow in a field. It is Witches' Hollow, and is green in winter and summer, and on moonlit nights witches have been seen dancing in it to the music of a fiddle played by an old black man. I never saw them, but I know people who saw witches dancing there.

"In a small house near the hollow, a little old woman lived who was a witch; she went by the name of Old Betty, and she danced on the green with the devil as a partner. There was an old man who lived in that neighborhood by himself; he was kind to Betty, giving her food and firewood. After a while he got tired of her and told her she must keep away. One day he caught her there and put her in a bag, and locked the bag in a closet, and put the key in his pocket, and went away to his work. While he was gone, she got out of the bag and unlocked the door. Then she got his pig, dog, cat, and rooster, put them into the bag, put the bag in the closet and hid herself.

"When the man came home the animals in the bag were making a dreadful noise. 'Ah, ha! Old Betty, there you are!' said the man. He took the bag and dashed it on his doorstone, and the old woman laughed and cried out, 'You haint killed Old Betty yet!'"

[Interesting though the above may be, it seems that Bliss

bowdlerized the story. In *The Narrow Land: Folk Chronicles of Old Cape Cod*, first published in 1934, Elizabeth Reynard— drawing on what she referred to as "oral traditions"— presented a racier version. *Her* Old Betty, whenever she stepped onto the enchanted Carver Green, became at once young and beautiful. The "old man" who was her neighbor was actually a not so old fellow by the name of Goodman Pease. Betty was always trying to entice him into joining her at the satanic revels on the Green. Though she didn't succeed in luring him into the devil's snare, she did succeed in seducing him. She got into the habit of visiting him on a daily basis; in return he gave her food and firewood. Eventually he tired of her, and that's when the trouble began.]

A nother story told by the old women was of two witches who lived in Plymouth woods, near the head of Buzzards Bay, who never went out in the daytime; but in the evening twilight they walked out "casting spells."

They cast a spell on a boy, compelling him to follow them home. Putting him to bed in a lower room, they went up a ladder into the loft. At midnight the boy saw them come down the ladder, go to the oven, and take out a quahog shell. Each witch rubbed it behind her ears and said "Whisk!" when each flew up the chimney.

The boy got up and rubbed the shell behind his ears; immediately he went up the chimney and found himself standing outdoors beside the witches, who were sitting astride black horses in the yard. On seeing the boy one of them dismounted, went into the house and returned with a "witch bridle" and a bundle of straw. She flung the bridle over the straw, and out if it came a pony. The boy was put on the pony's back, and away the three cantered across a large meadow, until they came to a brook. The witches cleared the brook at a leap; but the boy, when he cleared it, said to his pony, " A pretty good jump for a lousy calf!"

These words broke the spell; the pony vanished, and the boy stood alone with the bridle and the straw. He now ran after the witches, and soon he came to an old deserted house in which he heard the sound of fiddles. He peeped in a window and saw a black man fiddling, and the two witches and other old women dancing around him. Frightened, he ran down the road until he came to a farmhouse. He knocked on the door, was admitted, and the next day the farmer carried him to his parents.

[Reynard—again relying on "oral accounts"—presents background information on these two witches. They were not sisters, but had each—unbeknownst to the other—been married to the same man, at the same time. When they discovered his bigamous deceptions he prudently took to the sea. Each evening, at dusk, they went down to the shore hoping to catch sight of him so that, with their spells, they might change him into a sea serpent "and ride him from dusk to dawn."]

The old women who told the witch stories said that their grandmother had been personally acquainted with two witches, in the last century. One of these was named Deborah Borden, called at that day "Deb Burden," who was supposed to have caused a great deal of mischief in Wareham, Rochester, and Middleborough. It was thought to be necessary for farmers to keep in her good graces lest she should cause a murrain to come upon cattle, lest the rye refuse to head, and the corn to ear. She was a weaver of cloth and rag carpets. Woe to the unlucky housewife who worried Deb or hurried her at her looms!

I will let one of the sisters relate her story of this sorceress. It is not probable that the relater had ever heard of Robert Burns's story of Tam O'Shanter and his grey mare Meg; but a running brook filled the same place in that story and in this.

"Once my grandmother had a web of cloth in Deb's looms, so she sent my mother and a girl named Phoebe after it. The two girls were just as intimate as finger and thumb. They went to Deb's house and told her what my grandmother said, and it made her mad, 'cause she didn't like to be hurried. Near her back door was a tree full of red apples, and Phoebe said, 'Won't you please give me an apple?' and Deb said, 'Drat you! No, I won't!'

"My mother wasn't afraid, so she took an apple for Phoebe and one for herself, and she said to Deb: 'I ain't afraid of ye, ye old witch!'

"'Ye ain't?' Deb screamed. 'Then I'll make ye afraid afore ye git home!'

"They had a piece of woods to go through; in the middle of it there was a pair of bars, and on either side of the bars there was a brook. Suddenly they heard a roaring and they saw a black bull coming.

"'Oh!' said Phoebe, 'Captain Besse's bull has got out and he will get us.'

"So they ran for the bars. They got through them and across the brook, when the bull leaped the bars and stopped on the edge of the brook and roared; then my mother knew it was old Deb Burden who was in the bull to frighten the girls, because the brook stopped the critter. Witches can't cross running water, you know.

"The girls reached home dreadfully frightened, and they told what had happened. 'Never mind,' said my grandfather, 'I'll fix Debbie!'

"When she brought home the cloth, he came into the house and slipped behind her as she sat by the fire, and put a darning-needle through her dress and fastened her to the chair.

"Well, she sot; and every once in a while she said, 'I must go,' but she couldn't stir; she would be still for a while and the say, 'Why, I must go and tend my fire;' but she couldn't stir no more'n a milestone; and he kept her in the chair all day, and then he pulled out the needle and let her go.

"'Scare my gal agin, ye old witch!' he said. You know witches can't do anything when steel is nigh, and that was the reason the darning-needle held her.

"**O**nce Deb came to Thankful Haskell's in Rochester and sot by the fire, and her daughter, fourteen year old, was sweeping the room, and she put the broom under Deb's chair. You can't insult a witch more than that, 'cause a broomstick is what they ride on when they go off on mischief.

"Deb was mad as a March hare, and she cussed the child. Next day the child was taken sick, and all the doctors gin her up, and they sent for old Dr. Bemis of Middleborough; he put on his spectacles and looked at her, and said he, 'This child is bewitched; go, somebody, and see what Deb is up to.'

"Mr. Haskell got on his horse and rode to Deb's house; there was nobody in but a big black cat; this was the devil, and witches always leave him to take care of the house when they go out. Mr. Haskell looked around for Deb, and he saw her down at the bottom of the garden by a pool of water, and she was making images of clay and sticking in pins. As quick as he saw her he knew what ailed the child; so he laid his whip around her shoulders good, and said, 'Stop that, Deb, or you shall be burnt alive!'

"She whimpered, and the black cat came out and growled and spread his tail, but Mr. Haskell laid on the whip, and at last she screamed, 'Your young one shall git well!' and that child began to mend right off. The black cat disappeared all of a suddint and Mr. Haskell thought the earth opened and took him in."

"Moll Ellis was called the witch of Plymouth," said the other sister, taking up the story-telling. "She got a grudge agin Mr. Stevens, a man my grandfather worked for, and three years runnin' she cast a spell on the cattle and horses, and upset his hay in a brook. My grandfather drove and Stevens was on the load, and when they came to the brook the oxen snorted, and the horses reared and sweat, and they all backed and the hay was upsot in the brook.

"One day Stevens said, 'I'll not stand this; I'll go and see what Moll Ellis is about.'

"So he went up to her house, and there she lay on her back a-chewin' and a-mutterin' dretful spell words, and as quick as Stevens saw her he knew what ailed his cattle; and he walked right up to the bed, and he told Moll, 'If you ever upset another load of hay I'll have you hung for a witch.'

"She was dretful scart, and promised she would never harm him again. When she was talking, a little black devil, that looked like a bumblebee, flew into the window and popped down her throat; 'twas the one she had sent out to scare the cattle and horses.

"When Moll died, they couldn't get the coffin out the door because it had a steel latch; they had to put it out the window."

Whether Moll was in the habit of using the window to pass in and out of her dwelling-house in her lifetime, these women could not tell; but they firmly believed in Moll, and in witches, devils, and familiar spirits. That belief, under various names, still flourishes with certain classes of people in eastern Massachusetts. At Onset I have heard them speak of "manifestations" received from the spirits of the first settlers on the shores of Buzzards Bay, and I have read in a Bristol County newspaper that a mysterious hearse had been seen driven by a headless man along a road in the woods.

In regard to such stories I must say, as Mr. Addison said after relating the story of Glaphyra: "If any man thinks these facts incredible, let him enjoy his opinion to himself; but let him not endeavor to disturb the belief of others who by instances of this nature are excited to the study of virtue."

Addenda

The custom of notifying bees of a death in the family is evidently an ancient one, dating back thousands of years. Not only were hives trimmed with crepe following such a death, but they were often festooned with lengths of white ribbon in celebration of a wedding. The logic for these customs is simple: bees, an important source of nourishment, were considered to be sagacious creatures, and their care was often entrusted to one important family member. When this person died, it was believed that if the bees were not informed of the fact, they might suffer from neglect and perish, or simply swarm and leave the area.

John Greenleaf Whittier, esteemed New England poet and folklorist (1807-1892), published a ballad in 1858, "Telling the Bees," which as the title suggests exemplifies the ancient custom. In it a young man, visiting the farm of his beloved, Mary, sees a hired girl draping the bee hives in mourning ("draping each hive with a shred of black") and telling the bees of a death in the family ("I knew she was telling the bees of one / Gone on the journey we all must go!"). He assumes it is Mary's aged grandfather who has died, and is appalled when he hears the hired girl informing the bees that "Mistress Mary is dead and gone!"

Jane G. Austin includes an episode of "telling the bees" in her 1890 novel, *Dr. LeBaron and His Daughters*. Dr. LeBaron has been called to the bedside of a dying woman, whose remote farm "was on the outskirts of Marshfield, toward the sea...It was already twilight when he arrived at the lonely gray house, so squat to the ground and so surrounded with tentacle-like out-buildings and additions that it much resembled a great gray spider with all its legs extended in the effort of clinging to the ground, whence the raging autumn winds constantly sought to wrench it."

[The woman's husband greets him at the door.] "Come in, Doctor. I expect the woman's going tonight. Tide sets out 'bout three in the morning. It's making now, and fetching in ugly weather. It'll be a bad night for her to go. Seems as though anything as light as a sperit would blow away in such a gale..."

[Later, with the woman on the brink of death, her husband enters the room where for hours the Dr. has been keeping vigil by her side.]

"How is she?" whispered he.

"Very low. Going fast. She is unconscious."

"Can you tell how long?"

"Not precisely. Perhaps an hour."

"Tide turns at three."

"I cannot tell if she will wait for it."

"Well, I want to know very particular just a few minutes before she goes."

"I will call you, but probably she will not be conscious."

"That's no matter. I'd like to know *sure.*"

[Dr. LeBaron is touched by what he takes to be the husband's tender devotion. However...:] Once more the door opened, and a strange burly figure entered; it was indeed Quentin Wadsworth, but so disguised that LeBaron, for the moment, saw in him only the embodiment of his own fantastic visions. A yellow oilskin coat covered him from head to heel, and was girt about the middle with a red woolen scarf; a hat of the same material, and furnished with a cape falling upon the shoulders, was tied down bonnet-wise by a little plaid shawl...; a tin lantern, pierced with many holes, through which shone a dubious and broken light, was in his hand, and it was in a voice hoarse with emotion that he whispered: "Is she going? It's 'most three."

"Almost gone. Are you going for the minister...?"

[Wadsworth answers in the negative.]

"What, then?"

"Why, I'm going to tell the bees! Didn't you know why I was so pertikler about bein' called. If there's a death, and you don't tell the bees, first thing 'fore the breath's cold, they'll all leave early in the morning, and you'll never see them again."

...And as the old eight-day clock in the kitchen with moan and groan struck three, and the tide on Marshfield flats hung lifeless for a moment before it turned to the ebb, Lizzie Wadsworth's soul went forth to meet its Judge, and her husband, breasting the howling wind, hung over the beehives and chanted:

"Bees, I tell you of a death,

And bring you here the parting breath!

Death has come and death has gone:

Make your honey in the morn."

W hen Thankful Haskell's daughter placed the broom under Deb Burden's chair, the latter became "mad as a hare" because, Bliss's informants told him, she was highly insulted. But Deb may have had a greater reason for anger than mere insult, as this following example demonstrates: A witch "going to a neighbor's one day on an errand, prolonged her stay without apparent reason, till it was almost night. Though she was very uneasy all the time, and kept saying there was sickness at home and she ought to be there, still she didn't go. Finally, it was discovered that the broom had fallen across the door. When it was taken away, she fairly flew" —(from *Folklore in America*, edited by Tristram P. Coffin and Hennig Cohen). Brooms—the means by which witches transported themselves through the air— could also be used, like steel, to hold them captive.

The two women who lived in the Plymouth woods employed an alternative means of transportation: a "witch bridle," presumably similar to the one Mr. Wood of West Barnstable accused Liza Tower Hill of placing upon him before riding him to those nightly wild orgies by the pond in Plymouth (mentioned in the epigraph to this section). "Witch-riding served as a pastime and means of transport but also inflicted torment," Dorson informs us. "Tangible evidence of the practice lay in witch bridles, brightly colored strings full of curious knots." The bridles, tossed over straw, would cause ponies or other mounts to appear. All in all, though, witches preferred to use humans as mounts for their nocturnal outings. This belief is the origin of the term *hagridden*. People who woke up in the morning stiff and sore or with other body aches blamed it on witches. Again, an example from *Jonathan Draws the Long Bow*: "A rheumatic invalid explained his lameness by saying that old Sally Tripp turned him into a horse and drove him up and down Hurricane Hill every night beating him with a whip."

Witches' Hollow in Carver—"green in winter and summer"—typifies the sunken greens, or low-lying meadows (often located near graveyards or taverns or other places of ill repute) where witches (presided over by a fiddler, usually the devil in the guise of a black man—sometimes by a black-eyed sailor, or the devil decked out in red) purportedly gathered for dancing and revelry. Other staging areas for such nocturnal festivities included Hob's Hollow (Hob's Green) in Buzzards Bay and Plum Pudding Pond in Plymouth.◊

CRANBERRY Madness

The first draft of this memoir, written around 1984, appeared that year or the next in New Bedford: The Magazine of Southeastern Massachusetts; *some fifteen years later I incorporated a slightly different version into my first book of memoirs,* Deep Meadow Bog.

If, as literary critics and others are quick to point out, memory is faulty—and surely it is—then memoirs, which purport to be true, are of necessity at least in part fictional. The crucible of time performs a strange alchemy, converting the dull lead of facts into the glistening gold of reminiscence. That the final product may be iron pyrites—fool's gold—hardly seems to matter.

I know, for a fact, that there once was an old man named Monteej who, back in the 1940's and '50's, lived alone in a shack deep in the woods. I also know that he imagined himself—or pretended—to be a witch. What I don't *know for a fact is what really happened to him—or for that matter to Jay Jay and me— that September evening, now more than fifty years distant.*

Here the alchemy is not so much time *as it is youthful imaginations. What made sense then, to a nine-year-old, surely doesn't make sense now to a man in his sixties. And there is no arbiter of facts to turn to. Tragically, the only witness to those events, other than Monteej and myself, died decades ago in combat in Vietnam.*

A short while ago, to mark the fiftieth anniversary of the defeat of Geada, the ice demon, I returned to Deep Meadow Bog (what's left of it) and took a walk in the woods. At the spot where I think I remember Monteej's tarpaper shanty having stood there is now an inactive sand pit, long abandoned, and long since used as a dump for stumps and ditch mud and other debris.

The clutter strewn about that pit is a fitting metaphor for the "memoir" that follows.

After more than forty years I still cannot say for certain what happened the night Monteej challenged the ice demon Geada. Or whether anything happened at all.

At the time it all seemed very real. And there is a part of me that will always believe that what I remember of that night is exactly the way it was.

We were only children then. Jay Jay was ten years old and I was almost a year younger.

Jay Jay and I worked for Monteej. That is, we gathered the things he needed to make spells, and for the cures he brewed on his cast iron stove. He lived at the edge of the woods in a one-room tarpaper shack on property owned by the C.R. Barton Cranberry Company. Monteej was a *bruxe*, a male witch.

It was our job to supply Monteej with tadpoles and salamanders, the gauze strips of skin snakes leave behind when they shed, the bleached skulls of tiny rodents, sassafras and other roots and herbs, and anything else he commissioned.

We even stole for him; once the cigarette of a young Puerto Rican who insulted Monteej and scoffed at his sorcery, another time a button from the jacket of a Cape Verdean who mocked

Monteej and called him a bad name.

Jay Jay and I expected misfortune to fall upon both men. We were not disappointed. A few days after we removed the cigarette from its pack and handed it over to Monteej, the Puerto Rican was cut badly in a knife fight. And soon after the loss of his button the Cape Verdean, while mowing weeds along a ditch, slipped and fell on his scythe.

Jay Jay and I believed in Monteej and the power of his magic.

In August of that year the C.R. Barton Cranberry Company undertook an ambitious project, the installation of an underground sprinkler system.

In periods of drought the sprinkler system would irrigate Deep Meadow Bog and prevent the vines from drying out. It could also be used for the application of fertilizers and insecticides. But the sprinkler system's most important use would be against frost, in the spring when the vines are tender and the pink blossoms easily blasted, and in the fall when the ripening berries are vulnerable to the cold New England nights.

A tractor with a special plow dug the furrows in which the plastic pipe was laid. Uncle Dom and the other men pulled back the sod with potato diggers and covered the pipe, tamping down the soil under their feet. The work went fast and in less than a month the pipe was laid and the brass sprinkler heads were all in place.

On the day when the last head was screwed into place Uncle Dom hopped into his pickup and drove through the woods to the pump house on the Weweantic River. He took Jay Jay and me with him. We helped him prime the pump, filling buckets at the river's edge and carrying them up the slope to the pump house, where we emptied them into the shiny aluminum suction pipe.

"Once the pump is primed we shouldn't have to prime it again," Uncle Dom explained. "It should hold the prime all season."

Spitting on his hands for luck he pulled the electric switch.

The motor began to hum and we could feel it vibrate as the water surged up from the river and rushed along the pipe line toward Deep Meadow Bog.

Jay Jay and I scrambled into the pickup. Uncle Dom drove the fastest I had ever seen him drive over the rutted dirt road.

When we got to the bog the sprinkler heads were working, shooting water high into the air and drenching the berryladen vines. Uncle Dom whooped and Jay Jay and I dashed along the banks of the irrigation ditches, getting soaked to the skin in the heavy spray.

After the first excitement we got back into the pickup and helped Uncle Dom as he drove up and down the dikes looking for trouble spots.

Deep Meadow Bog is an old bog, one of the first to be built back in the nineteenth century. Laid out in the swamps where bog iron had been mined, it followed the contours where men and teams of oxen could clear away the boulders and tree stumps.

Monteej lived on a wooded knoll overlooking a half dozen acres separated by a strip of high ground from the rest of Deep Meadow Bog. When we drove up with Uncle Dom on the lookout for leaks and clogged sprinkler heads we could see Monteej in the doorway of his shack, staring at the strange spectacle of the ground spouting water in a hundred places.

The sprinkler system was completed just after Labor Day. School opened that week and Jay Jay and I had to set aside summer and Deep Meadow Bog and readjust to the regimen of blackboards and books.

One night during the second or third week of school I was awakened by a sharp tapping at my bedroom window. Dressing hastily, I crept through the dark house and let myself out by the back door.

Uncle Dom's pickup was missing from the driveway. I went around to the front and found Jay Jay waiting in the shadows of one of the maples that lined the street.

"Get your bike," he ordered, keeping his voice low. His own bicycle leaned against the trunk of the maple, splashed by moonlight filtering through the high branches. The air was still. Uncle Dom had said there was frost in it. He must have seen the mercury drop during the evening, or received a call from the Experimental Station in East Wareham. That would account for his pickup being gone.

Jay Jay lived with his parents in another part of town. Like Monteej he was Cape Verdean, and because his parents had been born on the islands he spoke the dialect of Portuguese known as Crioulo.

But that did not account for how he knew.

Monteej lived miles away, isolated, without electricity or telephone. He was old and lame and nearly blind. He seldom left his shack. There was no way he could communicate with Jay Jay.

But Jay Jay always knew when we were being summoned.

And because he always knew, and was almost a year older, I did not question him but ran and fetched my bike from the shed and pedaled after Jay Jay down the deserted streets.

The shack in which Monteej lived had only one window, facing the wooded side of the knoll, so that as Jay Jay and I approached we had only the moonlight to guide us. Resting our bicycles against the outer wall we knocked softly on the unlatched door and entered, Jay Jay leading the way.

Inside, the air was heavy, overheated, musty with old-man smells and the cures Monteej brewed on the cast iron stove. An oil lamp, its chimney cracked and blackened, cast a pallid glow on the bare walls and on Monteej himself as he sat on a pine rocker weaving spells in the air with his gnarled fingers. His face, wizened with age and years of hard toil, looked like a mask topped by tufts of white cotton.

He did not look up when we entered but sat gazing at the far wall, at the bare boards, at something only he could see. Jay Jay and I stood in the doorway, waiting.

Finally he spoke, his eyes fixed on Jay Jay and me, pinning us to the spot. His voice was low, the Portuguese syllables firmly wedded to the African and Asian cadences of his ancestors. He spoke for a long time. When he finished Jay Jay nodded, mumbled a few words in Portuguese, then turned to me.

"C'mon," he said, his voice quivering with fear or excitement, or a combination of both. "We got work to do."

He stepped outside and I followed, casting a backward glance as I slipped through the door. The flickering light from the oil lamp played tricks with my eyes. I thought I saw Monteej surrounded by dim shapes, half formed things, but when I blinked my eyes the shapes were gone.

Outside Jay Jay tugged at my sleeve.

"We gotta hurry," he whispered excitedly.

He ran around the corner of the shack to the lean-to where Monteej stored the wood he burned in his cast iron stove. Rummaging inside the lean-to, Jay Jay emerged into the moonlight clutching the ax Monteej used for chopping the wood.

"You know that hawk nest on the 'lectric light pole down by the pump house?"

I nodded. I could feel my body trembling. From the cold, I told myself. Not from fear. "There ain't any hawks in it now," I said, eyeing the ax. "What do we need that for?"

Jay Jay hefted the ax. "This is for after. We gotta cut some wood. But first we gotta climb that pole and get some hawk feathers out of that nest."

"What for?"

"C'mon. I'll explain on the way."

He dashed into the woods and I ran after him. Aided by moonlight we followed the old trail that led from the knoll down to the river.

"Monteej got the idea from that sprinkler system," Jay Jay explained, threading his way through the thick brush. He held the ax in his outstretched hands as a shield against the briars and brambles. "He says he spent his whole life thinking of a way, and now he's found it."

"Way to do what?"

"Get even," Jay Jay replied.

As I opened my mouth to speak a twig snapped back and lashed me across the face.

"Careful," I complained. "Even with who? For what?"

"For what happened when he was a kid." Jay Jay paused, as if unable to imagine Monteej as anything but an old man. "The island where he was born is near Africa. It hardly ever gets cold there. Only in the hills. He says that when he was a boy a great frost came and killed the crops. The people in the villages starved. His mother and father both got sick and died. Monteej almost died, too. He swore he would get even."

"Even with who?" I repeated.

We had reached the utility line that fed the pump house. The pole on which that spring a pair of hawks had nested and reared their young was just ahead.

Jay Jay lowered his voice. "Geada, the ice demon."

He climbed the pole while I held the ax. The night had grown colder. The air was still, as if frozen into silence. When he slid down the pole he was clutching a handful of feathers.

Picking out the four largest he discarded the rest. "Hold one in each hand, like this," he said. "That way he can't hurt us."

"Who can't?" I asked, seizing the two feathers he offered me.

Jay Jay stuffed the two remaining feathers into his pocket, grabbed the ax from my hands, and started toward the shack.

"Geada," he whispered over his shoulder. "The ice demon."

I gripped a feather tightly in each hand. "There's no such thing," I protested, hurrying to keep up with him.

"Yeah? Well, wait and see, smart ass. Monteej is gonna trick him. He's gonna catch Geada in a cage and kill him. And if he hears you talking, he might kill you, too."

I kept my mouth shut after that.

Jay Jay and I ran all the way, heedless of the thorns that tore at our clothes and of the roots that stretched out to play with our feet. As we ran I caught a glimpse of headlights a long way off, tearing through the swamp, and thought it must be Uncle Dom checking his thermometers.

I wished I was next to him in the cab of the pickup instead of dashing through the woods in aid of a witch.

About halfway up the knoll Jay Jay stopped and began cutting down maple seedlings. "We need a dozen," he said, trimming off the branches.

After seven or eight he got tired and I cut the rest. Holding the ax gave me courage.

"I would like to see anyone try messing with *me*," I told myself as I swung hard to part a young tree from its roots. "Demon or otherwise."

We lugged the saplings up to the shack two at a time. Monteej stood in the doorway watching us. He was bone thin, completely naked. His wrinkled skin, rubbed down with ointment, glistened in the moonlight like wet leather.

We built the cage according to the terse instructions Monteej gave to Jay Jay, erecting it at the edge of Deep Meadow Bog just outside the range of the nearest sprinkler head. We lashed the saplings together with pieces of twine Monteej had dipped in a potion and had put a spell on.

As soon as the cage was completed Monteej stepped inside, squeezing between two of the bars.

"He's the bait," whispered Jay Jay.

The moon had gone down by then; there was only starlight to see by—and the first faint hint of a dawn that was still hours away.

Monteej began to chant, slowly at first, then more rapidly, in a voice that was cracked and shrill. And suddenly the ground began to spurt. Uncle Dom had thrown the switch and the sprinkler heads were working, beginning with a low hiss like a hundred whispered sighs, growing stronger and merging into a loud hum as the water surged through the plastic pipe and the brass nozzles spun and the water shot into the air in wide arcs, slapping the ground at our feet.

It was then that shouting the words in a high-pitched voice Monteej sent out his challenge. A mist began to rise from the bog, a cold fog that enshrouded the cage with Monteej in it.

The mist made it impossible to see what was going on inside, but we could hear the cage shaking.

Yelling, "C'mon!" Jay Jay rushed at it, and I rushed after him. We hit the cage with our bodies and sent it spinning toward the bog, down into the irrigation ditch. That was the plan: Monteej would lure the ice demon into the cage, get him within range of the sprinkler heads, and then melt him down under the constant spray.

But something went wrong.

Engorged by the water and cold that were the source of its being, Geada the ice demon doubled and trebled in size, grew to gigantic proportions and triumphed over the crazed Monteej.

It was the hawk feathers, I guess, that saved Jay Jay and me from the demon's wrath. We were dazed, and could hardly walk, by the time Uncle Dom found us. But otherwise unharmed.

Monteej was missing. It was days later that Uncle Dom located the old man's body in a sand pit far from the cage and the shack.

"He must have wandered off. Confused," Uncle Dom speculated, ignoring the story of Geada that Jay Jay and I tried to relate.

Grandmother was so relieved to see me home safe and sound

that she forgot to punish me for sneaking out. Whatever story Jay Jay told his parents, they believed, or at least pretended to.

As for Jay Jay and me...We agreed that the less we talked about that night, the better for all concerned.◊

OtheR New England sorceries

Springfield has the distinction of having discovered the first recorded case of witchcraft in New England. Hugh Parsons was a somewhat cantankerous carpenter whose sharp tongue had made him enemies. Goody Parsons, his wife, no more sweet-tempered than her husband, made enemies on her own account. She was afflicted with occasional attacks of what we would today call insanity, which convinced her neighbors of her social intimacy with the devil. At her trial in 1651 she and her husband mutually accused each other of witchcraft, but both were acquitted of that charge...It was ten years later that witchcraft broke out at Hartford and Wethersfield, and forty years before the epidemic reached Salem. —Porter E. Sargent, A Handbook of New England

In 1794 it was asserted that no person had been hanged in Plymouth County "for above these sixty years past;" and a century before, in 1686, John Dunton wrote from Boston "there has not (it seems) been an execution here this seven years." —Charles Francis Adams, Massachusetts: Its Historians and Its History

Salem and Such

No inquisitor-in-chief ever gloated over the implements of the torture chamber with more morbid interest and pleasure than [Jonathan] Edwards gloated over that hell, upon the prolonged and exquisite torments of which he loved to dilate. His God was a horrible fetich, a demon of injustice, vengeance and wrath; and of a cruelty of disposition at once infinite and insatiable. And this frightful nightmare, this access of morbid suppression, Edwards deduced logically from the Scriptures; nor did it ever once occur to him that there must be something wrong in the premises which led to such an abhorrent result. In other words, he was the logical outcome of his environment—the system in which he had his being—and he represented it fairly. —Charles Francis Adams, Massachusetts: Its Historians and Its History

Numerous books, plays, and even poems have been written about the Salem witch trials. The following excerpt from *Myths & Legends of Our Own Land* by Charles M. Skinner neatly summarizes events pertaining to that seventeenth-century mania.

The extraordinary delusion recorded as Salem witchcraft was but a reflection of a kindred insanity in the Old World that was not extirpated until its victims had been counted by thousands. That human beings should be accused of leaguing themselves with Satan to plague their fellows and overthrow the powers of righteousness is remarkable, but that they should admit their guilt is incomprehensible, albeit the history of every popular delusion shows that weak minds are so affected as to lose control of themselves and that a whimsy can be as epidemic as smallpox.

Such was the case in 1692 when the witchcraft madness, which might have been stayed by a seasonable spanking, broke out in Danvers, Massachusetts, the first victim being a wild Irishwoman, named Glover, and speedily involved the neighboring community of Salem.

The mischiefs done by witches were usually trifling, and it never occurred to their prosecutors that there was an inconsistency between their pretended powers and their feeble deeds, or that it was strange that those who might live in regal luxury should be so wretchedly poor. Aches and pains, blights of crops, disease of cattle, were charged to them; children complained of being pricked with thorns and pins (the pins are still preserved in Salem), and if hysterical girls spoke the name of any feeble old woman, while in flighty talk, they virtually sentenced her to die. The word of a child of eleven years sufficed to hang, burn, or drown a witch.

Giles Corey, a blameless man of eighty, was condemned to the mediæval *peine forte et dure*, his body being crushed beneath a load of rocks and timbers. He refused to plead in court, and when the beams were laid upon him he only cried, "More weight!" The shade of the unhappy victim haunted the scene of his execution for years, and always came to warn the people of calamities.

A child of five and a dog were also hanged after formal

condemnation. Gallows hill, near Salem, witnessed many sad tragedies, and the old elm that stood on Boston Common until 1876 was said to have served as a gallows for witches and Quakers. The accuser one day was the prisoner of the next, and not even the clergy were safe.

A few escapes were made, like that of the blue-eyed maid of Wenham, whose lover aided her to break the wooden jail and carried her safely beyond the Merrimac, finding a home for her among the Quakers; and that of Miss Wheeler, of Salem, who had fallen under suspicion, and whose brothers hurried her to a boat, rowed around Cape Ann, and safely bestowed her in "the witch house" at Pigeon Cove. Many, however, fled to other towns rather than run the risk of accusation, which commonly meant death.

When the wife of Philip English was arrested he, too, asked to share her fate, and both were, through friendly intercession, removed to Boston, where they were allowed to have their liberty by day on condition that they would go to jail every night. Just before they were to be taken back to Salem for trial they went to church and heard the Rev. Joshua Moody preach from the text, "If they persecute you in one city, flee unto another."

The good clergyman not only preached goodness, but practiced it, and that night their prison was opened. Furnished with an introduction from Governor Phipps to Governor Fletcher, of New York, they made their way to that settlement, and remained in safe and courteous keeping until the people of Salem had regained their senses, when they returned. Mrs. English died, soon after, from the effects of cruelty and anxiety, and although Mr. Moody was generally commended for his substitution of sense and justice for law, there were bigots who persecuted him so constantly that he removed to Plymouth.

According to the belief of the time a witch or wizard compacted with Satan for the gift of supernatural power, and in return was to give up his soul to the evil one after his life was over. The deed was signed in blood of the witch and horrible ceremonies confirmed the compact. Satan then gave his ally a familiar in the form of a dog, ape, cat, or other animal, usually small and black, and sometimes an undisguised imp. To suckle these "familiars" with the blood of a witch was forbidden in English law, which ranked it as a felony; but they were thus nourished in secret, and by their aid the witch might raise storms, blight crops, abort births, lame cattle, topple over houses, and cause pains, convulsions, and illness.

If she desired to hurt a person she made a clay or waxen image in his likeness, and the harms and indignities wreaked on the puppet would be suffered by the one bewitched, a knife or needle thrust in the waxen body being felt acutely by the living one, no matter how far distant he might be. By placing this image in running water, hot sunshine, or near a fire, the living flesh would waste as this melted or dissolved, and the person thus wrought upon would die. This belief is still current among Negroes affected by the voodoo superstitions of the South.

The witch, too, had the power of riding winds, usually with a broomstick for a conveyance, after she had smeared the broom or herself with magic ointment, and the flocking of the unhallowed to their sabbaths in snaky bogs or on lonely mountain tops has been described minutely by those who claim to have seen the sight. Sometimes they cackled and gibbered through the night before the houses of clergy, and it was only at Christmas that their power failed them. The meetings were devoted to wild and obscene orgies, and the intercourse of fiends and witches begot a progeny of toads and snakes.

Naturally the Indians were accused, for they recognized the existence of both good and evil spirits, their medicine-men cured by incantations in the belief that devils were thus driven out of their patients, and in the early history of the country the red man was credited by white settlers with powers hardly inferior to those of the oriental and European magicians of the Middle Ages. Cotton Mather detected a relation between Satan and the Indians, and he declares that certain of the Algonquins were trained from boyhood as powahs, powwows, or wizards, acquiring powers of second sight and communion with gods and spirits through abstinence from food and sleep and the observance of rites. Their severe discipline made them victims of nervous excitement and the responsibilities of conjuration had on their minds an effect similar to that produced by gases from the rift in Delphos on the Apollonian oracles, their manifestations of insanity or frenzy passing for deific or infernal possession.

When John Gibb, a Scotchman, who had gone mad through religious excitement, was shipped to this country by his tired fellow countrymen, the Indians hailed him as a more powerful wizard than any of their number, and he died in 1720, admired and feared by them because of the familiarity with spirits out of Hobbomocko (hell) that his ravings and antics were supposed to indicate. Two Indian servants of the Reverend Mr. Purvis, of Salem, having tried by a spell to discover a witch, were executed as witches themselves. The savages, who took Salem witchcraft at its worth, were astonished at its deadly effect, and the English may have lost some influence over the natives in consequence of this madness. "The Great Spirit sends no witches to the French," they said.

Barrow Hill, near Amesbury, was said to be the meeting place for Indian powwows and witches, and at late hours of the night the light of fires gleamed from its top, while shadowy forms glanced athwart it. Old men say that the lights are still there in winter, though modern doubters declare that they were the aurora borealis.

But the belief in witches did not die even when the Salem people came to their senses. In the Merrimac valley the devil found converts for many years after: Goody Mose, of Rocks village, who tumbled downstairs when a big beetle was killed at an evening party, some miles away, after it had been bumping into the faces of the company; Goody Whitcher, of Amesbury, whose loom kept banging day and night after she was dead; Goody Sloper, of West Newbury, who went home lame directly that a man had struck his axe into the beam of a house that she had bewitched, but who recovered her strength and established an improved reputation when, in 1794, she swam out to a capsized boat and rescued two of the people who were in peril; Goodman Nichols, of Rocks village, who "spelled" a neighbor's son, compelling him to run up one end of the house, along the ridge, and down the other end, "troubling the family extremely by his strange proceedings;" Susie Martin, also of Rocks, who was hanged in spite of her devotions in jail, though the rope danced so that it could not be tied, but a crow overhead called for a withe and the law was executed with that; and Goody Morse, of Market and High Streets, Newburyport, whose baskets and pots danced through her house continually and who was seen "flying about the sun as if she had been cut in twain, or as if the devil did hide the lower part of her."

The hill below Easton, Pennsylvania, called Hexenkopf (Witch's Head), was described by German settlers as a place of nightly gathering for weird women, who whirled about its top in "linked dances" and sang in deep tones mingled with awful laughter. After one of these women, in Williams township, had been punished for enchanting a twenty-dollar horse, their sabbaths were held more quietly.

Mom Rinkle, whose "rock" is pointed out beside the Wissahickon, in Philadelphia, "drank dew from acorn-cups and had the evil eye." Juan Perea, of San Mateo, New Mexico, would fly with his chums to meetings in the mountains in the shape of a fire-ball. During these sallies he left his own eyes at home and wore those of some brute animal. It was because his dog ate his eyes when he had carelessly put them on a table that he had always afterward to wear those of a cat.

Within the present century an old woman who lived in a hut on the Palisades of the Hudson was held to be responsible for local storms and accidents. As late as 1889 two Zuñi Indians were hanged on the wall of an old Spanish church near their pueblo in Arizona on a charge of having blown away the rain clouds in a time of drought. It was held that there was something uncanny in the event that gave the name of Gallows Hill to an eminence near Falls Village, Connecticut, for a strange black man was found hanging, dead, to a tree near its top one morning.

Moll Pitcher, a successful sorcerer and fortune-teller of old Lynn, has figured in obsolete poems, plays, and romances. She lived in a cottage at the foot of High Rock, where she was consulted, not merely by people of respectability, but by those who had knavish schemes to prosecute and who wanted to learn in advance the outcome of their designs. Many a ship was deserted at the hour of sailing because she boded evil of the voyage. She was of medium height, big-headed, tangle-haired, long-nosed, and had a searching black eye. The sticks that she carried were cut from hazel that hung athwart a brook where an unwedded mother had drowned her

Moll Pitcher

child. A girl who went to her for news of her lover lost her reason when the witch, moved by a malignant impulse, described his death in a fiercely dramatic manner. One day the missing ship came bowling into port, and the shock of joy that the girl experienced when the sailor clasped her in his arms restored her erring senses. When Moll Pitcher died she was attended by the little daughter of the woman she had so afflicted.

John, or Edward, Dimond, grandfather of Moll Pitcher, was a benevolent wizard. When vessels were trying to enter the port of Marblehead in a heavy gale or at night, their crews were startled to hear a trumpet voice pealing from the skies, plainly audible above the howling and hissing of any tempest, telling them how to lay their course so as to reach smooth water. This was the voice of Dimond, speaking from his station, miles away in the village cemetery. He always repaired to this place in troublous weather and shouted orders to the ships that were made visible to him by mystic power as he strode to and fro among the graves.

When thieves came to him for advice he charmed them and made them take back their plunder or caused them to tramp helplessly about the streets bearing heavy burdens.

[According to Mary Bolté, in *Haunted New England*, John Dimond may still to this day be keeping a lookout for ships in danger. "Today when lightning flashes some say that if you are quick you can see a streak of purple move between the tombstones of the ancient graveyard. And perhaps a strange commanding roar is sometimes heard, although it could be just the thunder."]

"Old Mammy Redd, of Marblehead,
Sweet milk could turn to mould in churn."

Being a witch, and a notorious one, she could likewise curdle the milk as it came from the cow, and afterward transform it into blue wool. She had the evil eye, and, if she willed, her glance or touch could blight like palsy. It only needed that she should wish a bloody cleaver to be found in a cradle to cause the little occupant to die, while the whole town ascribed to her the annoyances of daily housework and business.

Her unpleasant celebrity led to her death at the hands of her fellow citizens who had been "worried" by no end of queer happenings: ships had appeared just before they were wrecked and had vanished while people looked at them; men were seen walking on the water after they had been comfortably buried; the wind was heard to name the sailors doomed never to return; footsteps and voices were heard on the streets before the great were to die; one man was chased by a corpse in its coffin; another was pursued by the devil in a carriage drawn by four white horses; a young woman who had just received a present of some fine fish from her lover was amazed to see him melt into the air, and was heart-broken when she learned next morning that he had died at sea.

So far away as Amesbury the devil's power was shown by the appearance of a man who walked the roads carrying his head under his arm, and by the freak of a windmill that the miller always used to shut up at sundown but that started by itself at midnight. Evidently it was high time to be rid of Mammy Redd.

Margaret Wesson, "old Meg," lived in Gloucester until she came to her death by a shot fired at the siege of Louisburg, five hundred miles away, in 1745. Two soldiers of Gloucester, while before the walls of the French town, were annoyed by a crow, that flew over and around them, cawing harshly and disregarding stones and shot, until it occurred to them that the bird could be no other than old Meg in another form, and, as silver bullets are an esteemed antidote for the evils of witchcraft, they cut two silver buttons from their uniforms and fired them at the crow.

At the first shot its leg was broken; at the second it fell dead.

On returning to Gloucester they learned that old Meg had fallen and broken her leg at the moment when the crow was fired on, and that she died quickly after. An examination of her body was made, and the identical buttons were extracted from her flesh that had been shot into the crow at Louisburg.

As a citizen of New Haven was riding home—this was at the time of the goings on at Salem—he saw shapes of women near his horse's head, whispering earnestly together and keeping time with the trot of his animal without effort of their own.

"In the name of God, tell me who you are," cried the traveler, and at the name of God they vanished.

Next day the man's orchard was shaken by viewless hands and the fruit thrown down. Hogs ran about the neighborhood on their hind legs; children cried that somebody was sticking pins into them; one man would roll across the floor as if pushed, and he had to be watched lest he should go into the fire; when housewives made their bread they found it as full of hair as food in a city boarding-house; when they made soft soap it ran from the kettle and over the floor like lava; stones fell down chimneys and smashed crockery. One of the farmers cut off an ear from a pig that was walking on its hind legs, and an eccentric old body of the neighborhood appeared with one of her ears in a muffle, thus satisfying that community that she had caused the troubles.

When a woman was making potash it began to leap about, and a rifle was fired into the pot, causing a sudden calm. In the morning the witch was found dead on her floor. Yet killing only made her worse, for she moved to a deserted house near her own, and there kept a mad revel every night; fiddles were heard, lights flashed, stones were thrown, and yells gave people at a distance a series of cold shivers; but the populace tried the effect of tearing down the house, and quiet was brought to the town.

[Mutilation of enchanted hogs was evidently not uncommon. In charge of the pigs kept by the almshouse in Portsmouth, New Hampshire, Molly Bridget was believed by the superintendent of the institution, a man by the propitious name of Clement March, to be a witch, and to have put a spell upon the animals in her care. March's first impulse was to burn Molly alive, but such a drastic measure might lead to a charge of murder, so instead he turned his attention to the pigs. He could, with impunity, immolate the pigs—but they were needed for food by the inmates of the almshouse. So he compromised by cutting off their tails, which he then cast into a bonfire he'd built for the purpose. As soon as the tails hit the flames Molly Bridget went into a violent seizure, as if suffering unbearable agony, and before the fire had died, so had she.]

In the early days of this century a skinny old woman known as Aunt Woodward lived by herself in a log cabin at Minot Corner, Maine, enjoying the awe of the people in that secluded burg. They moved around but little at night, on her account, and one poor girl was in mortal fear lest by mysterious arts she should be changed, between two days, into a white horse. One citizen kept her away from his house by nailing a horseshoe to his door, while another took the force out of her spells by keeping a branch of "round wood" at his threshold.

At night she haunted a big, square house where the ghost of a murdered infant was often heard to cry, and by day she laid charms on her neighbors' provisions and utensils, and turned their cream to buttermilk. "Uncle" Blaisdell hurried into the settlement to tell the farmers that Aunt Woodward had climbed into his sled in the middle of the road, and that his four yoke of oxen could not stir it an inch, but that after she had leaped down one yoke of cattle drew the load of wood without an effort. Yet she died in her bed.

Addenda

Samuel Adams Drake, writing in 1884, had this to say about Moll Pitcher: "...Lynn is likely to be celebrated throughout all time as having been the residence of the most successful fortune-teller of her day and generation—we might also say of whom we have any account in mystical lore, ancient or modern. While she lived she was without a rival in her peculiar art, and the prophetic words that she let fall were capable of being transmuted into gold...It was once said of Napoleon that he left a family, but no successor. Moll Pitcher left none in her wonderful gift of foretelling the future by practicing palmistry, or by simply gazing into the bottom of a teacup...Even the most incredulous were compelled to admit her predictions to be wholly unaccountable; while those who came to laugh went away vanquished, if not fully convinced.

"What is singular is that her reputation has rather increased than diminished with time. We have no account of her dupes, nor is there any 'Exposure' extant. It follows that the spot where for so many years Moll Pitcher so successfully practiced her art is the one to which the stranger first asks to be directed.

"Forty years ago there were very few firesides in New England that her fame had not reached, perhaps disturbed; and her successful predictions, alike astounding to the vulgar or to the enlightened, were the theme of many a midnight watch or forecastle confab. She was not, if we may credit local report, the [stereotypical] withered, decrepit, and toothless crone, but a woman who lived in the full gaze and gossip of a world which only accepted her claim to foreknowledge upon the unequivocal testimony of a thousand witnesses. Do you contend that her reputation was due solely to the shrewdness, penetration, and ready wit with which she was undoubtedly in a remarkable degree gifted? How, then, will you explain revelations of the future made ten and twenty years before the events predicted took place?

"When she was in the meridian of her fame and life the ordinary applicant saw a woman of medium stature, having an unusually large head, a pale, thin, and rather intellectual face, shaded by masses of dark brown hair, who was as thoroughly self-possessed as he was ill at ease, and whose comprehensive glance measured his mental capacity before he could utter a syllable. People of better discernment, who recollect her, say that her face had none of the wildness of the traditional witch, but was clouded with a habitual sadness, as of a mind overburdened with being the depository of so many confidences, perhaps crimes. She had a full, capacious forehead, arched eyebrows, eyes that read the secret thoughts of a suitor, a nose "inclined to be long," and thin lips—a physiognomy wholly unlike the popular ideal, but rather that of a modern Egeria—in the short, the witch of the nineteenth century.

"During the fifty years that she pursued her trade of fortune-telling, in what was then a lonely and little frequented quarter of the town, not only was she consulted by the poor and ignorant, but also by the rich and intelligent class. Love affairs, legacies, the discovery of crime, lotteries, commercial ventures, and the more common contingencies of fortune, formed, we may well imagine, the staple of her predictions; but her most valued clients came from the opulent seaports that are within sight of High Rock" [at the foot of which Moll Pitcher lived].

"The common sailor and the master, the cabin boy and the owner, equally resorted to her humble abode to know the luck of a voyage. It is asserted that many a vessel has been deserted when on the eve of sailing, in consequence of Moll's unlucky vaticination. She was also much besought by treasure-seekers— a rather numerous class in her day, whose united digging along the coast of New England would, if usefully directed, have reclaimed for cultivation no inconsiderable area of virgin soil. For such applicants the witch had a short and sharp reply.

"'Fools!' she would say. 'If I knew where money was buried, do you think I would part with the secret?'

"Moll Pitcher died in 1813, at the age of seventy-five. She was originally of Marblehead, and is said to have inherited the gift of prophecy from her grandfather, John Dimond."

Of Giles Corey, Drake had this to say: "Undoubtedly the most dramatic incident of this carnival of death was the trial and execution of Giles Corey, who, seeing the fate of all those who had preceded him, stubbornly refused to plead; and, to vindicate the majesty of the law he had thus defied, he was condemned to the atrocious *peine forte et dure* of the Dark Ages. The incredible sentence was carried out to the letter; and this miserable prisoner, while yet a living and breathing man, was actually crushed to death...This is the only instance of such a punishment being inflicted in New England.

"The heroic figure of this old man of eighty confronting judges and accusers in stoical silence is...unique in its grandeur...This amazing fortitude wrung from his enemies the title of the Man of Iron.

"The tradition was long current in Salem that at stated periods the ghost of Corey the wizard appeared on the spot where he had suffered, as the precursor of some calamity that was impending over the community, which the apparition came to announce. His shade, however, has long since ceased to revisit 'the glimpses of the moon,' and to do duty as a bugbear to frighten unruly children into obedience; but the memory of this darkest deed in New England annals is a phantom that will not be laid."

Innocent of the crime of witchcraft Giles Corey unquestionably was. But he may not have been entirely "blameless." Mary C. Crawford, in *The Romance of Old New England Rooftrees*, has this to say: "It is in connection with the witchcraft delusion in Salem that we get the one instance in New England of the old English penalty for contumacy, that of a victim's being pressed to death. Giles Corey, who believed in witchcraft and was instrumental in the conviction of his wife, so suffered, partly to atone for his early cowardice and partly to save his property for his children.

"This latter thing he could not have done if he had been convicted of witchcraft, so after pleading 'not guilty,' he remained mute, refusing to add the necessary technical words that he would be tried 'by God and his country.'

"The arrest of Mrs. Corey, we learn, followed closely on the heels of that of Tituba and her companions. The accused was a woman of sixty, and the third wife of Corey. She seems to have been a person of unusual strength of character, and from the first denounced the witchcraft excitement, trying to persuade her husband, who believed all the monstrous stories then current, not to attend the hearings or in any way countenance the proceedings. Perhaps it was this well-known attitude of hers that directed suspicion to her.

"At her trial the usual performance was enacted. The 'afflicted girls' fell on the floor, uttered piercing shrieks, and cried out upon their victim. 'There is a man whispering in her ear!' one of them suddenly exclaimed. 'What does he say to you?' the judge demanded of Martha Corey, accepting at once the 'spectral evidence.' 'We must not believe all these distracted children say,' was her sensible answer. But good sense was not much regarded at witch trials, and she was convicted and not long afterward executed. Her husband's evidence, which went strongly against her, is here given as a good example of much of the testimony by which the nineteen Salem victims of the delusion were sent to Gallows Hill.

" 'One evening I was sitting by the fire when my wife asked me to go to bed. I told her that I would go to prayer, and when I went to prayer I could not utter my desires with any sense, nor open my mouth to speak. After a little space I did according to my measure attend the duty. Some time last week I fetched an ox well out of the woods about noon, and he laying down in the yard, I went to raise him to yoke him, but he could not rise, but dragged his hinder parts as if he had been hip shot, but after did rise. I had a cat some time last week strongly taken on the sudden, and did make me think she would have died presently. My wife bid me knock her in the head, but I did not, and since she is well. My wife hath been wont to sit up after I went to bed, and I have perceived her to kneel down as if she were at prayer, but heard nothing.'

"Incredible as it seems today, this was accepted as 'evidence' of Mrs. Corey's bewitchment. Then, as so often happened, Giles Corey, the accuser, was soon himself accused. He was arrested, taken from his mill, and brought before the judges of the special court appointed by Governor Phipps to hear the witch trials in Salem. Again the girls went through their performance, again there was an endeavor to extort a confession. But this time Corey acted the part of a man. He had had leisure for reflection since he had testified against his wife, and he was now as sure that she was guiltless as that he himself was. Bitter, indeed, must have been the realization that he had helped convict her. But he atoned, as has been said, to her and to his children by subjecting himself to veritable martyrdom. Though an old man whose hair was whitened with the snows of eighty years, he 'was laid on his back, a board placed on his body with as great a weight upon it as he could endure, while his sole diet consisted of a few morsels of bread one day, and a draught of water the alternate day until death put an end to his sufferings.'"

Verrill describes a phase of those sufferings: "his eyes, during the fearful torture, 'did poppe from oute their sokettes' as a chronicler informs us, only to be 'presset back into place by ye Governor wyth his Staffe.'"◊

à New England Miscellany

The ghosts of long dead buccaneers loved to return to the bays and creeks where long ago, their treasures were safely stowed away, together with the corpses of the unfortunate seamen who had dug the hiding places. White Island off the New Hampshire coast is haunted by the ghost of Ann Brock who swore to stand guard over Blackbeard's treasure until the day of doom. —*Eric Maple,* The Realm of Ghosts

Witchcraft in Old and New England, by George Lyman Kittredge, a noted Harvard professor, was published in 1929. For a scholarly work it is quite readable, yet disappointing in this respect: despite its promising title and extensive coverage of the subject, it is disproportionally weighted toward the history of witchcraft and the persecution of witches in *Old*, rather than in *New*, England. And the material that is relative to New England deals primarily with the happenings in Salem. Scant attention is paid to the rest of the region.

Kittredge does mention an incident concerning a witch by the name of Lizzie Blatchford, who lived on Cape Cod in the early nineteenth century. He heard the story "about forty years ago" (i.e., sometime in the 1880's) from an eighty-four-year-old woman, who herself heard the story from one of Lizzie's victims. The incident took place on Mary Dunn Road, which Kittredge describes as formerly an old Indian trail, but "now a public highway" running from Barnstable Harbor straight across Cape Cod, named after an Indian woman "who once lived in a hut near a pond which the trail passess."

It seems that one day "old Mr. David Loring's wife" was riding on horseback from Hyannis to Barnstable along the trail. As she neared the pond "Lizzie Blatchford, a witch who lived on the margin, bewitched her horse, so that he insisted on going round and round the pond for a long time." Kittredge points out that Mrs. Loring was "pixey-led," and according to his research on the subject could easily have gotten out of her predicament. "Her remedy, if she had only known it, was to turn her cloak inside out and so reverse the spell."

A "spell" of another sort is recorded by Hattie Blossom Fritze in her 1966 book, *Horse and Buggy Days on Old Cape Cod*. Writing about her childhood in Osterville in the latter part of the nineteenth century, she recalls going for a long walk as a young girl in a secluded area on an island connected to the mainland by a drawbridge: "Well, I had no adventure, nor did I see a soul, not even the old witch who was left to guard the Captain Kidd treasure that was supposed to have been buried on the island."

Just how Captain Kidd had "left Hannah, or her spirit, to guard" the treasure Fritze does not say, though the time-honored method would have been to murder the person or persons who were to stand watch over the treasure and bury them along with it. The "guards" were often slaves or captives, or sometimes unsuspecting members of the crew (with, before being slain, the added indignity of having to lug the treasure to the burial spot and dig the hole). To establish a witch as spirit guard would be doubly effective against treasure-seekers, as this legend demonstrates: "It was said no one could speak while digging, as it would waken her, and her scream was terrifying." The curse notwithstanding, a couple of intrepid fellows managed somehow to locate the treasure. They "dug silently till suddenly a spade struck some object and one exclaimed, 'We've found it!' Immediately, there was a dull rumble, and the hole was empty! At the same instant a sharp screech overhead raised every hair on their heads, and they took to their heels."

Although Hannah "Screechum," as she was affectionately referred to by the good folk of Osterville, jealously guarded Captain Kidd's treasure, one New England witch actually assisted a pair of treasure hunters in their search for buried loot from a Spanish galleon.

John Gardner Brainard, editor of the *Connecticut Mirror*, affirmed that "It is a fact that two men from Vermont are now (July 11th, 1827) working by the side of one of the wharves in New London, for buried money, by the advice and recommendation of an old woman of that State, who assured them that she could distinctly see a box of dollars packed edgewise. The locality was pointed out to an inch; and her only way of discovering the treasure was by looking through a stone—which to ordinary optics was translucent."

Brainard celebrated the event with a lengthy poem, the first two stanzas of which are reprinted below:

The Money-Diggers

Thus saith the Book: "Permit no witch to live!"
Hence Massachusetts hath expelled the race;
Connecticut, where swap and dicker thrive,
Allowed not to their foot a resting place.
With more of hardihood and less of grace,
Vermont receives the sisters gray and lean,

Allows each witch her airy broomstick race,
O'er mighty rocks and mountains dark with green,
Where tempests wake their voice, and torrents roar between.

And one there was among that wicked crew
To whom the enemy a pebble gave,
Through which, at long-off distance, she might view
All treasures of the fathomable wave;
And where the Thames' bright billows gently lave
The grass-grown piles that flank the ruined wharf,
She sent *them* forth, those two adventurers brave,
Where greasy citizens their beverage quaff,
Jeering at enterprise, aye ready with a laugh.

Unfortunately for "those two adventurers," the witch omitted an important piece of information: like most buried treasures, this one was guarded.

Beneath the wave the iron chest is hot,
Deep growls are heard, and reddening eyes are seen;
Yet of the black dog she had told them not,
Nor of the gray wild geese with eyes of green,
That screamed and yelled and hovered close between
The buried gold and the rapacious hand.

So far as is known, the loot from the Spanish galleon lies there yet, in New London, Connecticut. Buried deep. And guarded well.

Still another buried treasure—also attributed to the ubiquitous Captain Kidd— figures as the subject of a ballad, also by a nineteenth-century newspaperman. Though not guarded by evil spirits, it is of interest because of its location: in Plymouth County, in the town of Carver. Henry S. Griffith mentioned the ballad in his *History of the Town of Carver* (published in 1913). In referring to the poem's author, Peg leg (uh, make that *Peleg*) McFarlin, Griffith wrote: "Perhaps the most noted of his poetical sketches was 'The Money Digger,' in which he related in three chapters the locally famous story of the finding of Capt. Kidd's treasure on the Island in Wenham Pond."

Lamentably, the "treasure" turned out to be part of an elaborate swindle, the only pirates involved being the crooks who duped others into believing it existed. But Peleg McFarlin, under the nom de plume of Ruralis, did write about one treasure, of sorts, that may have involved sorcery. It is worth repeating (abridged):

One tradition asserts that somewhere within the limits of our town exists a valuable Lead Mine, which would make him who should discover it a second Croesus. A certain man lived and died in Carver who had the good fortune to discover this mine. When he desired a few bullets for gunning purposes—being a sportsman—he would absent himself from home for an hour and return with an abundance of lead, which he would, by a simple process, run into bullets over his own fire. He fully intended, before his death, to confide the locality of the mine to a trusted friend. But, unfortunately, he departed this life very suddenly, and the mystery remains unsolved, though diligent search has been made.

We have, in our Carver woods, an elevation of land known as "Cannon Hill," and very few of our people doubt that at certain periods sounds have issued from this hill which resembled the resounding discharge of artillery; and some express the belief that in this very hill may be found the wonderful Lead Mine!

A year or two later, in a column he wrote regularly for the local *Gazette*, "Ruralis" returned to the subject of Cannon Hill and the enigma surrounding it. "Back in the woods, a mile or two from our village—strange, bleak, sepulchral place; timid, superstitious people dare not go near it; frightful noises issue mysteriously from its sides—generally in the night. Sounds of explosions, long and terrible, as if an artillery battle were in progress."

What was the real secret of Carver's Cannon Hill? Unfortunately, a year or so after penning the above, "Ruralis" ceased writing his column; to my knowledge, to this day the mystery remains unsolved, and like the matter of witchcraft has become with time more folklore than history.

R eturning to Professor Kittredge: in a later chapter of *Witchcraft in Old and New England* he briefly relates another incident involving Cape Cod. "Now and then," he writes, "a witch transforms a man into a horse by means of a magic bridle or otherwise, and rides him by night. About 1780 a young Cape Cod man was thus served by an old woman whose doughnuts he had stolen."

The "young Cape Cod man" was a sailor who stole the doughnuts while walking across the dunes to meet up with his ship in Provincetown. Coming upon a lonely cottage in the midst of the sands, he knocked at the door to ask for a bite to eat. When he received no answer he tried the door, found it unlocked, entered, and saw the doughnuts on the kitchen table. Being hungry he grabbed a few. The sole witness to his misdemeanor was a black goat.

Now, Goodie Hallett kept as a familiar, along with a black cat, a black goat—as did another witch, known only as The Witch of Truro. (According to Elizabeth Reynard, Sylvanus Rich, an elderly sea captain, had a slight contretemps with the latter, as a consequence of which she put a bit into his mouth, tossed a bridle and saddle onto him, "and all night long she rode him over the Truro hills.") Which of the two beldames bewitched the young sailor is not known. What is known is the manner of his bewitchment. Once his ship had put to sea he became ill. When questioned by his captain, he claimed that the witch whose doughnuts he purloined came to the ship, turned him into a horse and rode him at night, so that he woke up sore and exhausted. As proof he showed the captain his arm, which was black and blue where the witch had kicked him.

The captain, wise to the ways of witches, hit upon an immediate solution to the sailor's woes. Cutting the silver buttons from his coat, he fashioned them into bullets and loaded them into a gun, then gave the gun to the young man. That night a shot was heard, the sailor was found unharmed (though drenched in—presumably the witch's—blood), and that was the end of his troubles.

A stiff price to pay, though, for a handful of doughnuts.

Elsewhere in his book Kittredge mentions that as recently as 1897, in Lyme, Connecticut, "a rheumatic old woman was ducked by a mob 'to drive the devil out of her.'" But then, Connecticut seems to have had a time-honored tradition of persecuting witches. A. Hyatt Verrill, in *Along New England Shores*, mentions that "In 1651, with the outbreak of witchcraft persecutions, the people of Stratford decided they could not be without at least one witch, so they selected harmless old Goody Bassett as a promising victim, hanged her by her poor old neck and made a public spectacle of the execution."

Another author (W. Storrs Lee, in *The Yankees of Connecticut*) tells us that "Connecticut was infested with an ample number of witches, particularly around New Haven—hags that preceded horses through lonely stretches of road on moonlit nights, leaving only their riding hoods in the road as token of their actuality when help from the Almighty was summoned." Or they tormented children by (magically) sticking pins into their legs. Or, by demonic possession, they made hogs "run about on hind legs and squeal." As we've read, one enterprising hog farmer put a stop to that nonsense by slicing off the ear of one of the possessed animals. "Thereafter a suspected old woman about town always wore a muffler over the right side of her head."

Lee goes on to tell us that, despite such troubles, the witch situation wasn't all that bad. "Cautious Connecticut did away with only ten unfortunates during the whole period of the craze."

Not *too* shabby, I suppose: putting to death only ten innocent people.

Maine—perhaps because of its sparse population?—has an even better record. In 1692, in Wells, a man named "George Burroughs was prosecuted for witchcraft, the only case of witchcraft prosecution in Maine as far as I have been able to ascertain," Verrill tells us.

A dearth of prosecutions notwithstanding, Maine has had its share of witches, as—according to historian Herbert M. Sylvester—a fisherman from Kittery could well attest.

Skipper Perkins was a crusty old salt who made the mistake of insulting Old Betty Booker when she requested of him some halibut. In revenge, she first saw to it that he had bad luck fishing, so that "his schooner came home poorer than she went." Then in true witch fashion she set about making a bridle, and let it be known that "she was going to ride him down to York some wild night."

Terrified, the skipper hurried home each evening before dusk and double-barred his door and "quaked and shivered and shook until the sun came up." When Old Betty sent him word that, despite his efforts, come the first stormy night she was going to ride him to York, he went so far as to barricade the door by piling all his furniture against it.

To no avail. One night a fierce storm arose, and the door despite being double-barred and braced with furniture slowly began to open. Suddenly it "flew open and in trooped the witches. They pounced upon the skipper, and stripped him to his skin," whereupon Old Betty tossed on the bridle and climbed onto his back. Her companions piled onto her "and off they raced to York Harbor. When he lagged they pricked him with their claws," so that by dawn, when they returned to Kittery, he was "more dead than alive." It took him a full three weeks in bed to recover.

In addition to Old Betty Booker, the state of Maine can boast of Judith Howard, of Sebascodegan (an island in Casco Bay), who was skilled in the way of herbs—perhaps too skilled, for her enemies had the habit of suddenly falling ill and dying, as if poisoned; and a lass named Tessa, who lived near the banks of the St. John River, and whose mother was reputed to be a witch. There are many stories told of young Tessa, the most bizarre being about the time her mother's grave was exhumed (the townsfolk, for reasons unknown at this late date, were moving the cemetery). Although the body of the witch had lain in the ground for more than two years, it had suffered no ill effects, and appeared as it might have had it been buried only a few hours. Not one to miss an opportunity, Tessa tore off a piece of her mother's flesh (don't ask!) and brought it home in a bottle. She placed the bottle on a shelf under her mother's picture. From then on, around dusk, the picture would shed tears, and whenever the bottle was opened it would give off an odor of lilacs.◊

Bewitched, Bothered, and Bewildered
(from *What They Say in New England* by Clifton Johnson, 1896)

In the early part of the century, the people were very fond of telling ghost stories of an evening about the kitchen fire, and some people of great general intelligence were very superstitious. As an instance, I speak of Squire H., a man who was esteemed one of the pillars of the town. He said of his first wife that she saw her own apparition. One winter day she had been washing clothes in the kitchen. When she had finished she went to the glass, and combed her hair. When thus engaged she happened to look out the window and saw herself walking in the snow. The Squire had gone to the village, but when he returned he found his wife in tears. She told him what she had seen, and said she knew that such an appearance meant she was not to live long. She died within a year.

The Squire's second wife did not believe in witches, and never would accept this story; but the Squire explained her unbelief by stating that she was the first-born in her father's family, and that over such the witches had no power. All authorities agree that to see one's double is a very bad sign. Such affirm that Abraham Lincoln saw his double before he was assassinated, and that he told his friends he knew from that he would not live his term out.

The following is an example of an old-time witch story. It involves no less a personage than a clergyman. This clergyman's name was Hooker. He was traveling on horseback when, one evening, night overtook him at Springfield, Massachusetts, and he sought an inn. Other travelers were before him; and the landlord informed Rev. Mr. Hooker that he had only a single vacant room left, and, unfortunately, that room was haunted. The clergyman said he did not mind that, and took the room.

He had retired, and everything was still when twelve o'clock came, and with it the witches. In they flocked through keyholes and cracks, until they filled the room. The visitors brought with them many shining dishes of gold and silver, and prepared for a feast.

When everything was ready they invited the clergyman to partake. Although he knew very well that if he ate with witches he would become one, he accepted the invitation.

"But," he said, "it is my habit to ask a blessing before eating;" and at once began it.

The witches couldn't stand blessings, and fled helter-skelter, leaving feast and plate in possession of the preacher. Whether he ate the whole feast himself or not is not related. At any rate, Rev. Mr. Hooker secured the gold and silver dishes; and the next morning, while he was continuing his journey, a crow flapping along overhead shouted to him, "You are Hooker by name, and Hooker by nature; and you've hooked it all."

Bewitched Cream

D aniel Smith was churning. He looked into the churn now and then to see what progress he was making, but the butter was no nearer coming the last time he looked in than it was the first. The suspicion grew on Mr. Smith that there was something uncanny about this fact. The more he thought about it the more certain he became that there was a witch in the cream.

To expel this evil spirit he dipped up a little of the cream, and threw it into the fire. Immediately after that the butter came. That same day it was reported that Widow Brown had burned herself. Then Mr. Smith knew it was the Widow Brown who had bewitched his cream.

[Something similar happened in the town of Scituate, in Plymouth County. "A certain woman...was accused of bewitching people's soap. To drive her out of the soap a black-handled butcher knife was once stabbed into the soap, and the soap-maker claimed that it cut off the witch's ear, so that she wore a shawl over head ever afterwards to conceal the wound."—E. Victor Bigelow, *A Narrative History of the Town of Cohasset*]

Raising the Wind

"M y father," said the narrator, "worked for a man in Longmeadow, Mass. The man he worked for was the doctor there. One day the doctor says he guessed he'd send some rye to the mill. But the wind didn't blow none so't they could winnow it. In them times they used to have to shake it outdoors somewhere so't the wind'd blow the chaff away. There warn't a mite of wind stirring that morning; and so the doctor, he and my father, sot there in the kitchen a-talking, and guessing they'd have to let it go till next day.

"While they was doing this in comes the doctor's wife, and says the wind was beginning to blow up a little. And sure enough! when they come to go out the wind was blowing considerable, and my father went right to cleaning up the rye. There might not be nothing to it, but my father always thought that woman was a witch. 'Twarn't natural the wind should come up sudden that way, without no help. That woman she wanted the flour, and so she just went out and made the wind blow up the way it did."

The Cat Which Lost a Claw

There was a man by the name of Jones had a sawmill. He was so driven with work that he frequently was obliged to run the saw evenings. One night he was going down to the mill to work; and his wife said she didn't want him to, but he went just the same. He got the saw running, and a log rolled on, when along came a black cat he'd never seen before. She purred around very friendly, rubbing up against the man, and trotting along on the log he was sawing. Finally she got to fooling around the saw, and got a claw cut off. Then she ran away up toward the man's house. When the man got through work, and went home, he found his wife had one of her fingers done up. He asked her what the matter was, and she wouldn't tell him. But he kept at her, and after a while she let him see her hand. One finger was cut clean off. Then the man knew his wife was a witch, and that she was that same black cat which got its claw sawed off at the mill.

[Witches, it seems, were always getting themselves into trouble by the practice of transformation: changing themselves into, or taking on the form of, an animal. The loss of an ear or a hand was sometimes the least of their woes. Let the following, as passed on by Marillis Bittinger, serve as a cautionary tale for any budding witches.

In Eastham, on Cape Cod, a sea captain named Jed Knowles married a "young, lovely, and devoted bride." For many years she accompanied him on his voyages. But eventually, for whatever reasons, and despite her pleas, he decided she was better off left at home and he sailed without her. He did this several times, always with his wife's objections, until one voyage, when "much to the captain's surprise and delight, Mrs. Knowles did not demur, and offered no argument..."

He sailed away, unaware that a mouse had followed him aboard.

Soon members of the crew began to complain that the ship's supplies were being nibbled upon. And one night, unable to sleep because of rustling and scampering noises in his cabin, the captain lit a lamp and discovered a tiny mouse—unafraid—staring at him. This went on for several nights, with Captain Knowles tolerating, and even growing somewhat attached to, the mouse. That is, until the tiny creature ate the captain's supper and did other damage, such as gnawing at his log, and otherwise making a nuisance of itself. Finally, in a fit of anger, the captain grabbed a cat-o'-nine-tails, lashed the mouse to death, and tossed it out his porthole.

When he arrived home he found his wife dead, in a pool of sea water, and with whip marks upon her body.]

How To Kill a Witch

I t was a common trick in the olden time of such women as were witches to turn into cats, and go scooting along the top rails of fences. It was useless trying to shoot these witch cats with any ordinary load. Leaden bullets would not touch them. To kill them, the gun had to be loaded with a silver ball. It was needful for the person who went witch-killing to use great care about his ammunition; for they said about the ball, that,—

"If it isn't pure silver
It only maims and doesn't kill her."

The Wilbur Witches

These witches made themselves famous about seventy-five years ago in the hill country of western Massachusetts.

Their pranks were played in a secluded hamlet known as Simpson Hollow, and they particularly afflicted the Wilbur family there. The Wilburs were a good, respectable, church-going family; but, by some mysterious dispensation of Providence, they were the ones who had to suffer. They would find their Sunday clothes snipped and gashed, for one thing. While this witch business was going on, the Wilburs made it a point to look over the clothes they had hung up in the closets and about the rooms each day. One morning, after Mrs. Wilbur had made the rounds, she is reported to have said, "Well, I believe there's nothing this time." The words were no sooner out of her mouth than a skirt dropped down on the floor with a half-yard slash in it.

Granny Bates, who was one of the family, one day missed her gold beads, and where should they be found but at the top of the well-sweep.

Again the beads were gone. They searched high and low; and finally the beads were found in a teacup, in the bottom of a tub of clothes that they had taken down by the brook to rinse, and spread on the grass.

Another strange thing was that the family were continually finding odd articles of one sort and another in the dye-tub by the kitchen fireplace. This could not be allowed to go on, and one of the boys was told to sit on the dye-tub and stay there;

but nothing came of it.

These stories circulated through the neighborhood, and occasioned not a little excitement. Even the minister was a good deal exercised over it. He led a number of prayer-meetings at the house; but the Devil continued, nevertheless, in apparent full possession.

Sometimes a watch was set, and this served to fasten suspicion on Granny Bates and an old cat owned in the family. When someone went to get meal to sift, they found this old cat in the bin. Then they noticed that the old cat had begun to look very strangely, and there were those who affirmed that its features bore a very close resemblance to those of Granny Bates.

At last, on one of the nights when a party was trying to drive out the witches, this old cat was seen to go through a closed garret window, glass and all, without breaking a pane. People who saw it said that this was no other than Granny Bates in the form of a cat. But it was never settled who the witch really was, and some had suspicions of a servant-girl who was working in the family. It was a good while before the excitement died out; and for a long time after, when anything strange happened in the community, people would say, "Well, that's the Wilbur witches."

Note

In an earlier chapter we read of how old Meg from Gloucester was killed by two silver bullets, and in this chapter we learned a useful ditty regarding the importance of the purity of the silver used to manufacture the bullets. *Folklore in America* reinforces the notion: "If a witch should bewitch you, she will probably appear to you next time as an animal. Shoot the animal with a silver bullet if you desire to injure the witch." (Those of us who fondly remember the werewolf movies from the 1940's, in which silver bullets were effectively put to use against the lycanthropic antihero, have already taken this advice to heart.)

Granny Mott, of Westerly, Rhode Island, likewise met her end by means of a silver bullet. One evening, for reasons best known to herself, she harrassed a group of children who were attempting to harvest berries before a frost could destroy the crop. In the form of a heath hen (usually a docile creature) she swooped from the sky and plucked berries from the children's baskets. Wise to the ways of witches, their father rushed into the house, loaded his musket with a silver coin, and dashing outside shot the bird dead. Sure enough, the next day Granny Mott lay dead beneath the ice, "the water weaving strands of her thin gray hair over staring eyes, while in the middle of her forehead was the glint of something silver."—(*Haunted New England*)

Incidentally, Granny's bizarre death was, in a sense, poetic justice, in that while alive she was wont to cross the Pawcatuck River from Westerly to the Connecticut shore, walking across the ice when the river was barely frozen. On numerous occasions she was seen to whirl "across a floe far too frail to hold even...children."

One final "Witch Meets Death by Means of Silver" story:

In Exeter, Rhode Island, a woman reputed to be a witch decided to marry a wealthy farmer. Though no prize himself (other than the fact that he was rich), he knew better than to get mixed up with a witch and refused her advances. Enraged, she took the form of a cat and began to torment him. At which juncture he seized a silver mug, tore off its handle, and "plunged the jagged piece of silver into the cat's gullet." Next morning, guess whose corpse was found in the farmer's field, blood oozing from a gaping wound in her throat.◊

the partriöge Witch

(from *Myths & Legends of Our Own Land* by Charles M. Skinner, 1896)

Two brothers, having hunted at the head of the Penobscot until their snow shoes and moccasins gave out, looked at each other ruefully and cried, "Would that there was a woman to help us!"

The younger brother went to the lodge that evening earlier than the elder, in order to prepare the supper, and great was his surprise on entering the wigwam to find the floor swept, a fire built, a pot boiling, and their clothing mended. Returning to the wood he watched the place from a covert until he saw a graceful girl enter the lodge and take up the tasks of housekeeping.

When he entered she was confused, but he treated her with respect, and allowed her to have her own way so far as possible, so that they became warm friends, sporting together like children when the work of the day was over.

But one evening she said, "Your brother is coming. I fear him. Farewell." And she slipped into the wood.

When the young man told his elder brother what had happened there—the elder having been detained for a few days in the pursuit of a deer—he declared that he would wish the woman to come back, and presently, without any summons, she returned, bringing a toboggan-load of garments and arms. The luck of the hunters improved, and they remained happily together until spring, when it was time to return with their furs.

They set off down the Penobscot in their canoe and rowed merrily along, but as they neared the home village the girl became uneasy, and presently "threw out her soul"—became clairvoyant—and said, "Let me land here. I find that your father would not like me, so do not speak to him about me."

But the elder brother told of her when they reached home, whereon the father exclaimed, "I had feared this. That woman is a sister of the goblins. She wishes to destroy men."

At this the elder brother was afraid, lest she should cast a spell on him, and rowing up the river for a distance he came upon her as she was bathing and shot at her. The arrow seemed to strike, for there was a flutter of feathers and the woman flew away as a partridge. But the younger did not forget the good she had done and sought her in the wood, where for many days they played together as of old.

"I do not blame your father: it is an affair of old, this hate he bears me," she said. "He will choose a wife for you soon, but do not marry her, else all will come to an end for you."

The man could not wed the witch, and he might not disobey his father, in spite of this adjuration; so when the old man said to him, "I have a wife for you, my son," he answered, "It is well."

They brought the bride to the village, and for four days the wedding dance was held, with a feast that lasted four more days. Then said the young man, "Now comes the end," and lying down on a bear skin he sighed a few times and his spirit ascended to the Ghosts' road—the milky way. The father shook his head, for he knew that this was the witch's work, and, liking the place no longer, he went away and the tribe was scattered.◊

facts, fancies, and fantasias

To find a horseshoe in the road is a sign of good luck. Many of the poorer farmhouses of New England have a horseshoe tacked up over an outer entrance for good luck.

In times past, and those not very far removed, the object of the horseshoe over the door was to keep out the witches.—Clifton Johnson, What They Say in New England

In some countries they nail a wolf's head to the door, to prevent and cure all mischiefs by charms and witchcrafts.—Reginald Scott, The Discovery of Witchcraft, *1665, as noted in* A Treasury of Witchcraft

Quakers, Witches, and Other Blasphemers

At the close of the King Philip War it was solemnly asserted from at least one pulpit that the war had been caused by the behavior of boys in the meeting-houses. The war was the punishment of the Plymouth Colony for the "disorder and rudeness of youth in many congregations in time of the worship of God, whereby sin and profaneness is greatly increased." — Elroy S. Thompson, History of Plymouth, Norfolk and Barnstable Counties

...a fit of madness was regarded as a manifestation of the immediate presence of the Deity. At first the acute attacks of the mania took the forms of ordinary religious persecutions, finding vent against Baptists and Quakers; then it assumed a much more interesting phase in the Salem Witchcraft craze of 1691-92. The New England historians have usually regarded this curious and interesting episode as an isolated phenomenon, to be described as such, and palliated it by references to the far more ferocious and unthinking maniacal outbreaks of like nature in other lands

at about the same time. This is simply to ignore its significance.
—*Charles Francis Adams,* Massachusetts: Its Historians and Its History

Cotton Mather claimed that Satanism lay at the heart of Quakerism, and suggested that the sect's members had been lured into the dogma by the devil himself. —*Sally Smith Booth,* The Witches of Early America

Bitter were the persecutions endured by Quakers at the hands of the Puritans. They were flogged if they were restless in church, and flogged if they did not go to it. Their ears were slit and they were set in stocks if they preached, and if any tender-hearted person gave them bed, bite, or sup, he, too, was liable to punishment. They were charged with the awful offense of preaching false doctrine, and no matter how pure their lives might be, the stern Salemite would concede no good of them while their faith was different from his.—Myths & Legends of Our Own Land

In contrast to the Pilgrims of Plymouth, who did not vigorously persecute persons accused of witchcraft, the Puritans of Massachusetts Bay enacted harsh laws and inflicted severe punishments on those they perceived to be in league with the devil (i.e., anyone who held beliefs different from their own). "The most inhuman and cruel punishments and tortures in the whole history of our country were imposed upon men and women by the Puritans for the crime of professing a belief in any religion other than [their own]," A. Hyatt Verrill asserts, with some justification, in *Along New England Shores.*

By 1692, before the Salem hysteria, a total of forty-four cases of witchcraft and three hangings had already occurred in that colony. In *The Intellectual Life of Colonial New England*, the historian Samuel Eliot Morison cites one example which occurred in 1688: "Four children...went into fits and accused an old woman with whom they had had an altercation about the family wash of having bewitched them. The poor creature confessed she had made a compact with the devil, and was discovered to have the traditional witch apparatus of rag dolls representing the victims, which she stroked or pinched to torment them." Needless to say she was put on trial for witchcraft, found guilty, and executed.

The following illustrates certain aspects of the Puritanical world view, in particular its intolerant attitude toward Quakers as well as those perceived to be witches.

(from *The Sabbath in Puritan New England* by Alice Morse Earle, 1891)

Though the Puritans were such decorous, orderly people, their religious meetings were not always quiet and uninterrupted. We know the torment they endured from the "wretched boys," and they were harassed by other annoying interruptions. For the preservation of peace and order they made characteristic laws, with characteristic punishments. "If any interrupt or oppose a preacher in season of worship, they shall be reproved by the Magistrate, and on repetition, shall pay £5, or stand two hours on a block four feet high, with the inscription in Capitalls, 'A WANTON GOSPELLER.'"

As with other of their severe laws the rigid punishment provoked the crime, for Wanton Gospellers abounded. The Baptists did not hesitate to state their characteristic belief in the Puritan meetings, and the Quakers or "Foxians," as they were often called, interrupted and plagued them sorely. Judge Sewell wrote, in 1677, "A female quaker, Margaret Brewster, in sermon-time came in, in a canvass frock, her hair disheveled loose like a Periwig, her face as black as ink, led by two other quakers, and two other quakers followed. It occasioned the greatest and most amazing uproar that I ever saw."

More grievous interruptions still of scantily clad and even naked Quaker women were made into other Puritan meetings; and Quaker men shouted gloomily in through the church windows, "Woe! Woe! Woe to the people!" and, "The Lord will destroy thee!" and they broke glass bottles before the minister's very face, crying out, "Thus the Lord will break thee in pieces!" and they came into the meeting-house, in spite of the fierce tithingman, and sat down in other people's seats with their hats on their heads, in ash-covered coats, rocking to and fro and groaning dismally, as if in a mournful obsession.

Quaker women managed to obtain admission to the churches, and they jumped up in the quiet Puritan assemblies screaming out, "Parson! thou art an old fool," and, "Parson! thy sermon is too long," and, "Parson! sit down! thee has already said more than thee knows to say well," and other unpleasant, though perhaps truthful personalities.

It is hard to believe that the poor, excited, screaming visionaries of those early days belonged to the same religious sect as do the serene, low-voiced, sweet-faced, and retiring Quakeresses of today. And there is no doubt that the astounding and meaningless freaks of these half-crazed fanatics were provoked by the cruel persecutions which they endured from our much loved and revered, but alas, intolerant and far from perfect Puritan Fathers. There poor Quakers were arrested, fined, robbed, stripped naked, imprisoned, laid neck and heels, chained to logs of wood, branded, maimed, whipped, pilloried, caged, set in the stocks, exiled, sold into slavery and hanged by our stern and cruel ancestors.

Perhaps some gentle-hearted but timid Puritan souls may have inwardly felt that the Indian wars, and the destructive fires, and the earthquakes, and the dead cattle, blasted wheat, and wormy peas, were not judgments of God for small ministerial pay and periwig-wearing, but punishments for the heartrending woes of the persecuted Quakers.

Others than the poor Quakers spoke out in colonial meetings. In Salem village and in other witch-hunting towns the crafty "victims" of the witches were frequently visited with their mock pains and sham fits in the meeting-house, and they called out and interrupted the ministers most vexingly. Ann Putnam, the best and boldest actress among those cunning young Puritan witch-accusers, the protagonist of that New England tragedy known as the Salem Witchcraft, shouted out most embarrassingly, "There is a yellow bird sitting on the minister's hat, and it hangs on the pin in the pulpit."

Mr. Lawson, the minister, wrote with much simplicity that "these things occurring in the time of public worship did something interrupt me in my first prayer, being so unusual." But he braced himself up in spite of Ann and the demoniacal yellow bird, and finished the service. These disorderly interruptions occurred on every Lord's Day, growing weekly more constant and more universal, and must have been unbearable. Some few disgusted members withdrew from the church, giving as reason that "the distracting and disturbing tumults and noises made by persons under diabolical power and delusions, preventing sometimes our hearing and our understanding and profiting of the word preached; we having after many trials and experiences found no redress in this case, accounted ourselves under a necessity to go where we might hear the word in quiet."

These withdrawing church members were all of families that contained at least one person that had been accused of practicing witchcraft. They were thus severely intolerant of the sacrilegious and lawless interruptions of the shy young "victims," who received in general only sympathy, pity, and even stimulating encouragement from their deluded and excited neighbors.

Notes

Quakers not only did not persecute witches, they actively protested against the folly of so doing. George Fox, the Society's founder, in an address to seafaring men in 1676, said: "For you may see that it was the Lord who sent out the wind and raised the mighty storm in the sea, and not your witches, or ill-tongued people, as you vainly imagine." (For more on the raising of winds and storms by witches, see the chapter titled "Black Cats, Bats, and Pointed Hats.")

Quakers themselves, however, were sometimes accused of being witches: "For the Quaker revelation doth arise in them only when the witchcraft fit is upon them."◊

Malpractice and Its Consequences

"The first woman to be executed for witchcraft in Massachusetts was Margaret Jones, 'physician and doctoress.'" —*Elroy S. Thompson,* History of Plymouth, Norfolk and Barnstable Counties

Women were more frequently accused of the crime of witchcraft than were men. Of the twenty innocents in Salem who were found guilty and executed, only six were males—"only" being of course relative; an injustice is an injustice, regardless of the sex of the victim.

In colonial days women were far more vulnerable than men. They had far fewer rights, whether in regards to the ownership of property, or in choosing the leaders of the community, or in choice of a career. Except in cases involving such issues as infanticide or abortion (where a physical examination of the accused might be necessary), they were not allowed to serve on juries. As a consequence they had less power than men, and fewer means of protecting themselves.

Essentially, only a handful of "careers" were open to woman. Midwifery was one of them. Midwifery, however, was fraught with dangers. To begin with, women who possessed healing skills were looked upon with suspicion. Whence came those skills? From consorting with the devil perhaps? Consider: midwives make use of herbs. Witches, too, make use of herbs.

And what if, despite the midwife's best efforts, the child or the mother or both should die before during or after delivery? *Someone* must be at fault. Perhaps the midwife had it in for the family, and used her nefarious knowledge to bring about the death of child or mother.

An incident in the early history of Plymouth Colony, though it does not deal with witchcraft, illustrates the dangers routinely faced by midwives and the hostility they sometimes unwittingly provoked—(and, coincidentally, involves Quakers).

(from "The Physicians" by Palo Alto Pierce, in *A History of the Town of Freetown*)

Early in the beginning of the seventeenth century we hear of an old midwife called Granny Brightman, whose circuit of practice was very extensive. She lived in the southern part of Freetown, near Slade's Ferry. On one occasion we find her in Beech Woods in Lakeville, pressing onward in a severe snow storm to the assistance of a suffering sister. Her horse gave out and she called upon Isaac Peirce (who had squatted there) for a fresh one, but he refused her and allowed her to pursue her journey as best she could.

This was not the end of it, however, for when Isaac Peirce—who was a Quaker, and had left the Massachusetts Bay Colony on account of the bitter feeling which still continued there toward those professing that faith—next went to the Friends' Quarterly Meeting at Swansea, whom should he find there but Granny Brightman? She had come to enter complaint against him for refusing her assistance in her time of need, and after a patient hearing it was determined as the sense of the meeting, that he should make to her a formal and humble acknowledgment of his fault, which he accordingly did.

Granny Brightman was fortunate in that she dealt with Quakers rather than Puritans. Margaret Jones, of Charlestown, was not so lucky. Hers is the distinction of being the first person executed in Massachusetts for witchcraft. The evidence that led to her hanging was overwhelming: she had "a malignant touch," often causing people with whom she came into contact to fall violently ill; she was a "practicing physic" who used herbs to effect her cures; she admonished patients who did not follow her advice that they would not get well, and lo and behold, they often did not; and "some things which she foretold came to pass accordingly."

In other words, despite the fact that she was treating severly ill people, who no doubt sought medical assistance only as a last resort, her patients often got well. Margaret Jones's crime was that she was too skilled.

The greatest danger, it appears, that midwives or other female practitioners of medicine faced was that of succeeding too well. For example, in 1669 Goody Burt stood accused of being a witch for the simple reason that she so often cured her patients. Surely it was not her competence and knowledge that accounted for her success rate; she must have had supernatural help. (It should come as no surprise to learn that her chief accuser was another—less successful—physician.)

Despite the particular dangers faced by women, male physicians were not entirely exempt from the suspicions of the ignorant, as the following excerpt from *Dr. LeBaron and His Daughters* illustrates:

There were those who whispered that "the French doctor" had bequeathed to his son uncanny secrets bordering upon art magic; that the herbs he so carelessly culled in the fields, or cultivated in the lush garden stretching down behind his house to the Town Brook, were components of the Elixir Vitæ whose formula the doctor was always striving to reproduce. They said that he sought for the Philosopher's Stone; they said all the things their forefathers had said in the beginning, of Faustus, and Grandier, and Galileo, and many another man too learned and too reticent for the comprehension of his neighbors. Lucky was it for Lazarus LeBaron that he lived in an age when these beginnings of gossip had ceased to lead to any deadly end, and were perhaps rather an advantage than a danger to their object.

None the less was the student very careful of allowing any, even the nearest and dearest of his household, to inquire too curiously into the occupations or the instruments confined within those sacred walls, and it was no doubt some resolution to continue this reserve that formed itself in the man's mind, as, leaning an elbow on the mantelshelf, his eyes wandered from the relics upon their harrateen background to the crucibles at his feet.◊

Black Cats, Bats, and Pointed Hats

*In the British Isles particular attention was paid by the witches,
in their description, to the tall hat worn.* —Pennethorne Hughes,
Witchcraft

Whether it be the black silhouette of a woman astride a
broom, as depicted on famed Witch Rock in Rochester,
Massachusetts, or a cartoon character from Disney, the familiar,
stereotypical witch is easily recognized by her sharp features (in
particular her prominent chin) and by her distinctive outfit.

The tall, pointed hat of the witch of fashion has its origins in
antiquity; like the wizard's hat, it derives from the hood worn by
elves and fairies and other mythological creatures of the
primordial woods. At first its color was green, but as witches
and other pagans became associated with the devil it took on the
more ominous shade of black.

The linking of cats with witches is of a later date, though not
much later than the latter part of the Middle Ages, when cats
were first introduced into Europe. The reasons for associating
cats with witches should be rather obvious: lonely and pathetic
old women, living apart from fellow humans, whose only

companions were their cats, were most frequently targeted as being witches; and cats are by their nature mysterious creatures —who slink around at night, and whose eyes change shape and appear to glow in the dark.

"It was a common trick in the olden time of such women as were witches to turn into cats," Clifton Johnson reported, in *What They Say in New England: A Book of Signs, Sayings, and Superstitions*. Certainly we've seen sufficient examples of such transformations, "The Cat Which Lost a Claw" being fairly representative.

Of all varieties, black cats—the color of midnight—are the ones most often associated with evil. We saw in Plymouth how Mother Crewe's black cat, presumably doing her bidding, brought about the death of Southward Howland (sending him literally southward, that is, to hell). On lower Cape Cod Goodie Hallett's black cat, along with her black goat, rode on the backs of porpoises. According to Elizabeth Reynard, whenever seamen from that area "saw two green eyes staring from the spume, [they] exclaimed: 'Thar be Goodie Hallett's familiar waitin' to pick up souls." And rough weather was sure to follow.

It's no secret that black cats were (and are) considered unlucky. Even now, many otherwise sensible people cringe when one crosses their path, though no one of my acquaintance goes so far as to turn back home to restore good fortune, as was formerly recommended. (Virgins, it seems, were in particular peril. "If a black cat walked before an unwed maid, precaution suggested that she gather a handful of grass and scatter it as she followed." —Elizabeth Reynard, *The Narrow Land*)

Black cats were generally believed to possess special powers; they were used for magical purposes even by those who would not have considered themselves—by any stretch of the imagination—witches. On Nantucket for instance, according to Eleanor Early in *An Island Patchwork*: "To keep their [seafaring] sweethearts at home, the girls [for the most part Quakers] put black cats under tubs. Pussy's predicament was supposed to make a head wind, strong enough to keep a ship from sailing. And if the cats had nine lives, maybe they could spare one for love." It's possible the Nantucket girls learned the trick from the aforementioned Goodie Hallet, who could prevent a ship from leaving port by placing her black cat under a "berry-bushel." Her doing so resulted in either a dead calm or unfavorable winds.

(Nantucket women had good reason to want to delay the departure of their sweethearts. A man on a whaling voyage might be gone for a very long time, as exemplified by the following from Verrill's *Along New England Shores*: "To the whaleman, a year's cruise was just a little jaunt, and there is the story of one Nantucket captain who, when reminded by his mate that he had not kissed his wife goodbye, retorted, 'Why should I? I'm only going on a two-years' cruise.'")

The belief that cats could be instrumental in creating winds and brewing up storms is centuries old. The following, titled "Raising a Storm with a Cat," is excerpted from the pamphlet *News from Scotland* (1591) and is just one among a number of similar citations found in *A Treasury of Witchcraft* compiled by Harry E. Wedeck: "John Fian, master of the school at Saltpans, Lothian, ever nearest to the devil...chases a cat... In which chase he was carried high above the ground, with great swiftness, and as lightly as the cat herself...Asked to what effect he chased the creature, he answered that in a conversation... Satan commanded all that were present to take cats... he chased the said cat, to raise winds for destruction of ships and boats."

Similarly in Scotland, in 1591, an elderly, well-educated woman named Agnes Sampson confessed (like Fian, under severe torture) to having, a year earlier, raised a storm for the purpose of wrecking a ship in which King James was sailing. She effected the storm by binding to a cat various parts of a dead man's body, then tossing the cat into the sea.

Less pernicious beliefs about cats and the weather abound. A cat that claws at a cushion or carpet, or merely appears nervous, "is said to be raising a wind. This belief is popular everywhere at sea, and is widely believed in sea coast towns on Cape Cod..." —from *A Treasury of American Superstitions* by Claudia de Lys. The same source states that "to throw a cat overboard raises a storm at sea."

The way a cat washes itself can also affect the weather. "If a cat washes herself in the usual manner, the weather will be fair, but it will be bad if she licks herself above the ears."

This latter belief was held by my own dear mother—who was not otherwise notably superstitious—though in all fairness, she did not believe that the cat's behavior *caused* the rain, rather that it merely *foretold* it. Countless times, from early childhood on, I heard my mother declare: "It's going to rain. The cat just washed over his ear." From my own experience I must say there appears to be some foundation to the notion of cats as prognosticators of inclemency, though whether cats feel inclined to wash over their ears because of changes in atmospheric conditions, or moisture levels in the air, or from some other natural cause, I leave for those of a more scientific bent to decide.

Finally, one old forecasting technique holds that when a cat lies on its back there will be a storm.

Black cats had other uses, too. In a short story originally published in one of the pulp magazines from the 1930's ("Philtered Power," by Malcom Jameson), the list of a necromancer's ingredients for making magic potions includes "Gall of black cat. Killed in a churchyard on St. John's Eve; Moon new, Mars ascendant."

Blood from the lopped off tail of a black cat was a sure cure for shingles and other diseases of the skin. It is said that until recently, in Ireland, it was "almost impossible to find a black cat with but the shortest stump of a tail, because they have been gradually cut off bit by bit for their healing power." —Dorothy Jacob, *Cures and Curses*

Perversely—or perhaps just *withershins* (i.e., in a course opposite to the normal)—a witch in Long Compton, England, according to J.A Brooks in *Ghosts and Witches of the Cotswolds* "would, or could, only assume the form of a white animal— sometimes a rabbit, a cat, or even a mouse." The same author tells us that another witch of the Cotswolds, called Nance, "could turn herself into a white cat..." Presumably witches as white cats—as opposed to black ones—are a regional peculiarity. Reinforcing that notion is a spectral white calf often seen "on the road to Ettington which is also haunted by an old woman who wears a white sun bonnet and carries a basket." Perhaps calf and woman are one and the same.

In effecting cures, the precise color of the cat was essential. Not just any old cat would do. For example, Dorothy Jacob tells us that "Tortoise-shell cats, always lucky, would cure warts with hairs from their tails, but only in the month of May." In witchcraft, it's the little details that count.

Who among us has not been awakened at night by the caterwauling of amorous felines? Sometimes witches made use of cats merely to annoy and harass their victims. One witch harried her neighbors at night with "a number of cats, who would suddenly appear in the room, frolic over the beds, and then disappear just as mysteriously as they had come, since the house was shut up for the night and there was no opening through which animals their size could enter or leave" (*Folklore in America*).

◇◇◇

Pirates, buried treasure, and black cats—what a combo! Now that we're well versed in the lore of all three, we can—perhaps—relish the following (from *Myths & Legends of Our Own Land*).

Harry Main (a dark-souled being, who, after a career of piracy, smuggling, blasphemy, and dissipation, became a wrecker and lured vessels to destruction with false lights) was believed to have buried his ill-gotten wealth in Ipswich, and one man dreamed for three successive nights that it had been interred in a mill. Believing that a revelation had been made to him he set off with spade, lantern, and Bible, on the first murky night—for he wanted no partner in the discovery—and found a spot he recognized as the one that had been pictured to his sleeping senses. He set to work with alacrity and a shovel, and soon he unearthed a flat stone and an iron bar. He was about to pry up the stone when an army of black cats encircled the pit and glared into it with eyes of fire.

The poor man, in an excess both of alarm and courage, whirled the bar about his head and shouted "Scat!" The uncanny guards of the treasure disappeared instanter, and at the same moment the digger found himself up to his middle in icy water that had poured into the hole as he spoke.

The moral is that you should never talk when you are hunting for treasure. Wet, scared, and disheartened, the man crawled out and made homeward, carrying with him as proof of his adventure a case of influenza and the iron bar. The latter trophy he fashioned into a latch, in which shape it still does service on one of the doors of Ipswich.

As with cats, bats (mysterious, nocturnal, in some instances blood-sucking) have long been associated with witches; they were once popularly known as "the witches' bird." Witches—

like their comrades in evil, vampires—sometimes took on the shape of a bat when going about their nefarious business.

Furthermore, an old homily warns: "If a bat flies low enough to touch your head, you will die." This did not seem to faze the eccentric Charles Wade, who practiced witchcraft in Snowshill Manor (in the Cotswolds) and "who slept with an enormous preserved bat over his bed." In what manner the bat was preserved is not specified.◊

high in the Sky

Though seemingly innocuous, many nursery rhymes can be traced back to events or customs that were both evil and horrible. The familiar "Eenie, meenie, minie, mo," by which children select a person or object, may have its origin in druidic rites of human sacrifice. And "Ring-a-ring-a-roses, a pocket full of posies, achoo, achoo, we all fall down" is believed by some to refer to the Black Plague ("roses" and "achoo" referring to the symptomatic rash and sneezing, respectively; posies to prophylactic herbs; and "we all fall down" to the inevitable fate of the plague's victims).

So it may not constitute too great a stretch of the imagination to propose that the following nursery rhyme, attributed to Mother Goose, may in fact conceal a reference to witchcraft.

> There was an old woman tossed up in a blanket,
> Seventy times as high as the moon,
> What she did there, I cannot tell you,
> But in her hand she carried a broom.
> Old woman, old woman, old woman, said I!
> Whither, O wither, O whither so high?

To sweep the cobwebs from the sky,
And I shall be back again by and by.

First, a word about Mother Goose: The original "Mother Goose," teller of nursery tales or fables, was probably a French creation dating back to the late Sixteen Hundreds; whereas the American "Mother Goose" who was a singer and compiler of nursery rhymes was one Elizabeth Foster, born in Boston on April 5, 1665. In 1692 (coincidentally the year of the Salem witch madness) she became, at the age of twenty-seven, the stepmother of ten children when she married Isaac Goose. She and Isaac had a daughter, Elizabeth, who married a printer named Thomas Fleet.

The elder Elizabeth—Mother Goose—spent much of her time in the nursery singing to her grandchildren the nonsense rhymes she herself had learned as a child. In 1719 Thomas Fleet gathered together these songs and ditties and published them in a broadsheet titled *Mother Goose's Melodies*.

Although, living in Massachusetts in the latter seventeenth and early eighteenth centuries, Elizabeth Goose would have been all too well acquainted with the concept of witchcraft, I am not suggesting that she consciously repeated a poem about a witch. I am suggesting, however, that the nursery rhyme may have originated—somewhere in the dim past—as a reference to witchcraft.

The significance of the broom is obvious, witches being known to use brooms for transportation after first anointing them, and themselves, with oils.

And why would an old woman be tossed in a blanket, if not as a means to force her to confess to the crime of being a witch? Throughout the Middle Ages—even into the eighteenth century—tens of thousands, perhaps hundreds of thousands (some estimates place the figure in the millions) of innocent men and women were executed as witches. In nearly every instance they were forced by torture to confess to their crime. The tortures they were forced to endure were hideous. I'll bypass the more gruesome and mention only some of the lesser forms.

The following (from *The Encyclopedia of Witchcraft and Demonology*) is all too typical, and occurred in England in 1603: "The men punched her" [an eighty-year-old woman] "with the handles of their daggers, *tossed her in the air*, flashed gunpowder in her face, and 'having prepared a stool in which they had stuck daggers and knives with sharp points upwards, they often times struck her down upon the same stool whereby she was sore pricked and grievously hurt.'"

I find "tossed in the air" significant. Then again, *quien sabe?* Perhaps the poem is merely whimsical, and not at all related to witchcraft.◊

that Demon, Rum

The woman's accuser, a local tavern keeper, maintained that soon after an argument with the defendant, he was attacked by several shadowy animals with gleaming eyes. The story not only demonstrates that supernatural specters were part of colonial witchlore, but also gives some credence to the theory that in heavy-drinking Early America, visions of specters were sometimes the result of delirium tremens. —Sally Smith Booth, The Witches of Early America

This town seems to have been affected with the evil early and hard. Its taverns, located about midway between the rum importing towns of New Bedford and Plymouth with stages making their periodical stops...Drunkeness everywhere...even at funerals the inebriety of those in official capacities shocked the sensibilities of the mourners.— Henry S. Griffith, History of the Town of Carver

The witch hunt meant good business for Nathaniel Ingersoll. A bill run up on March 1, the first day of the examinations of Tituba, Sarah Good, and Sarah Osborne, shows the marshals, constables, and assistants spending three shillings on food and two shillings on cider. The constables laid out an extra ninepence on cider and sixpence on rum.—Frances Hill, Hunting for Witches

Drinking to excess was a common failing in early New England; our forebears liked their liquor and they liked it hard. Members of the clergy were particularly prone to drunkenness. The reason for this lack of sobriety among preachers was simple. Besides preaching on the Sabbath and officiating at weddings and funerals, ministers were expected to periodically make the rounds within their community: not only visiting the sick and infirm, the dying or newly born, the troubled in spirit; but also paying social calls to their parishioners, especially the prominent, the well-to-do and influential.

When the parson called, it was ill-mannered not to offer him a drink (considering that he might have ridden his horse, or even walked, a number of miles, in foul and inclement weather). And equally ill-mannered for him to decline. By the fifth or sixth visit of the day the unfortunate pastor might very well be staggering drunk—yet still feel obliged to accept his next parishioner's offering.

Alcoholism and witchcraft. Can there be a connection?

Is it possible that not a few of the "bewitchings" witnessed or otherwise experienced in colonial times were due to the effects—hallucinations, *delirium tremens*—of over drinking? Pure speculation—or so I at first thought, until completing the research that resulted in this chapter and discovering that at least one historian, Sally Smith Booth, had already voiced a similar opinion. Not so implausible, then, given the popularity—and the availability—of alcoholic beverages, both homemade and purchased.

In *The Sabbath in Puritan New England*, Alice Morse Earle

writes, "Cider sold in 1782 for six shillings...a barrel... A hundred years previously—in 1679—cider was worth ten shillings a barrel. That this thawed-out Sunday barrel of cider would prove invariably a source of much refreshment, inspiration, solace, tongue-loosing, and blood-warming to the chilled and shivering deacons, elders, and farmers who gathered in the noon-house, anyone who has ever imbibed that all-potent and intoxicating beverage, oft-frozen 'hard' cider, can fervently testify."

(Earle describes and explains the importance of the noon-house: "...a long, low, mean, stable-like building with a rough stone chimney at one end." It was also known as a "Sabba-day house or horse-hows. It was a place of refuge in the winter time, at the noon interval between the two services, for the half-frozen members of the pious congregation, who found there the grateful warmth which the house of God denied.")

"Sometimes a very opulent farmer having built a noon-house for his own and his family's exclusive use, would keep in it as part of his 'duds' a few simple cooking utensils in which his wife or daughters would re-heat or partially cook his noon-day Sabbath meal, and mix for him a hot toddy or punch, or a mug of that 'most insinuating drink'—flip.

"Flip was made of home-brewed beer, sugar, and a liberal dash of Jamaica rum, and was mixed with a 'loggerhead'—a great iron 'stirring stick' which was heated in the fire until red hot and then thrust into the liquid. This seething iron made the flip boil and bubble and imparted to it a burnt, bitter taste which was its most attractive attribute. I doubt not that many a 'loggerhead' was kept in New England noon-houses and left heating and gathering insinuating goodness in the glowing coals, while the pious owner sat freezing in the meeting-house, also gathering goodness, but internally keeping warm at the thought of the bitter nectar he should speedily brew and gladly imbibe at the close of the long service."

Reinforcing the notion of our Puritan forebears as heavy imbibers, Earle has this to say: "The minister's ordination was, of course, an important as well as spiritual event in such a religious community as was a New England colonial town. It was always celebrated by a great gathering of people from far and near, including all the ministers from every town for many miles around; and though a deeply serious service, was also an excuse for much merriment ...the ordination-ball was always a great success. It is recorded that at one in Danvers a young man danced so vigorously and long on the sanded floor that he entirely wore out a new pair of shoes...

"There was always given an ordination supper—a plentiful feast, at which visiting ministers and the new pastor were always present and partook with true clerical appetite. This ordination feast consisted of all kinds of New England fare...and an inevitable feature at the time of every gathering of people, from a corn-husking or apple-bee to a funeral—a liberal amount of cider, punch, and grog...which latter compound beverages were often mixed on the meeting-house green or even in punch-bowls on the very door-steps of the church. Beer, too, was specially brewed to honor the feast...Portable bars were sometimes established at the church-door, and strong drinks were distributed free of charge to the entire assemblage."

In *The Old Coast Road from Boston to Plymouth*, Agnes Edwards has this to say: "There are countless church records which duplicate this one of the ordination of a Massachusetts pastor in 1729: '6 Barrels and a half of Cyder, 28 gallons of wine, 2 gallons of Brandy, and 4 of rum, loaf sugar, lime juice and pipes,' all, presumably, consumed at the time and on the spot of the ordination."

The ministry were not the only professionals at risk. Doctors might also be prone to excessive imbibing, though perhaps not more so than the general populace. Too much merrymaking did get one Cape Cod doctor into serious trouble—trouble involving a witch, and quite possibly the devil.

Although he was well educated, and respected for his medical skills, Dr. Richard Bourne of Barnstable was known for his fondness for liquor. As he grew older, his visits to the local taverns became more and more frequent. On Christmas night, 1810 (as recounted in *The Narrow Land*), he spent the greater part of the evening celebrating at a party in Hyannis. The festivities ended at midnight; the doctor, far into his cups and still singing his favorite song, "Old King Cole," lurched into the saddle and began the moonlit ride on his horse in the frigid cold to his home, four miles distant, by way of the woods.

(Dr. Bourne's unfortunate choice of song may have contributed to his misadventure. According to no less an authority than Cotton Mather, Old King Cole himself used to attend the wild gatherings of witches that New England was so noted for. "Old King Cole" was the tune to which, folks said, witches and the devil danced and made merry.)

Somewhere on his homeward journey Dr. Bourne's horse, taking a wrong turn, ventured onto the path that led to Half Way Pond, an area associated with witches. Suddenly the doctor encountered an eerie glow. Dismounting to investigate, he discovered the source of the weird light: a phosphorescent stump. What happened next is unclear. Did the doctor, as malicious tongues would have it, spend the remainder of the night carousing with the ghost of Liza Tower Hill (whom we've already met—the witch who years earlier had caused Mr. Wood of West Barnstable so much rheumatic pain by tossing a bridle onto him and riding him at night to Plum Pudding Pond in Plymouth)? And having spent the night with Liza, did Dr. Bourne shake hands with the devil and, unthinking, come close to selling his soul to the fiend? Then, coming to his senses, did the doctor in his fright mount his horse so quickly that he forgot his boots by the glowing stump?

Or, as the less superstitious maintained, did Dr. Bourne—his mind befuddled with drink—mistake the glow of the phosphorescent stump for that of a cheerful fire, and stop and pull his boots off in order to warm his feet? And then, still in a drunken stupor, remount his horse and ride off, forgetting the boots and leaving them behind?

Whatever the case, he became disoriented, and was found the next day lost and riding without his boots.

After that he became the butt of jokes and cruel pranks, and having lost his reputation, died poor and alone.

The story of one drunken doctor and his imagined encounter with a witch proves very little, of course. But if nothing else, alcohol may have contributed to the muddled thinking that in earlier times led to the heinous torture and execution of so many harmless and innocent victims. Or perhaps not. Perhaps I'm reading too much into the old records. In either case, it's interesting to learn of the role that demon rum played in the lives of our god-fearing (though far from teetotaling) forebears.

Notes

There is nothing to be feared in a phosphorescent birch stub, even with the drip of rain from the leaves making stealthy, ghostly footfalls all through the wood and the voice of the east wind in the trees overhead beginning to take up a querulous, wordless complaint that moved back and forth with the footfalls. Foxfire is a common enough phenomenon. It is easy to explain it all as I do now. The strange part of such things is always that, at the time, no matter what a man's training and experience, he feels creeping back and forth in his bones the old, pale terror of primitive man. —Winthrop Packard, Old Plymouth Trails

The old pale terror. How many of our fairy tales, our hauntings, our sworn accounts of bewitchings, can be attributed to that "common enough phenomenon," foxfire? Consider the following, from *Major Bradford's Town: A History of Kingston 1726-1976.* "Colonel Gray arrived in Plymouth in 1643 and was very successful in his land and business dealings—he was the richest man in the colony when he died in 1681. After his death "nearby residents sighted mysterious moving objects in the swampy pasture he had owned...More scientific minds might suspect the object and noises were the phenomena of marsh-gas, but the legend calls it Colonel Gray on his horse."◊

InÖians anÖ WitchcRaft

It was in very deed a fearful time. The old gossips of the neighborhood gathered together every evening around some large, old fashioned fireplace, where, with ghastly countenances whitening in the dim firelight, the marvelous legends which had been accumulating for more than half a century in the wild woods of the new country, were related, one after another, with hushed voices and tremulous gestures. The mysteries of the Indian worship—the frightful ceremonies of the Powwaw—the incantations and sorceries of the prophets of the wilderness, and their revolting sacrifices to the Evil Being, were all made subjects of these nocturnal gatherings. —John Greenleaf Whittier, Legends of New-England in Prose and Verse, *1831*

In *Witchcraft in Old and New England*, Professor Kittredge makes a cogent observation (of a fact which, once it has been pointed out, seems obvious, but which is often forgotten or overlooked): "There was a very special reason," he states, "why troubles with the powers of darkness were to be expected in New England—a reason which does not hold good for Great Britain or, indeed, for any part of Western Europe. I refer, of course, to the presence of a considerable heathen population —the Indians."

In the view of not only the colonists but of the rest of the world as well, the native population—non-Christian—were pagans, and therefore by definition devil-worshipers. Indians were known, during their religious ceremonies, to invoke spirits. Their medicine men (powwows or, in the spelling derived from the Narraganset version, *powwaws*) made no secret of the fact that they considered themselves to be wizards.

Referring to the powwaws of Martha's Vineyard, Matthew Mayhew (who died in 1710) wrote: "Their practice was to either by desiring the Spirit to them appearing to perform what mischief they intended; or to form a piece of leather like an arrowhead, tying an hair thereto; or using some bone, as of a fish (that it might be known Witchcraft, to the bewitched) over which they performed certain ceremonies; and dismissed them to effect their desire." In other words, the medicine men either commanded a conjured up demon to harm someone directly, or they employed a voodoo-like device that depended, in part, on the victim's fear to be effective. In either case they were performing sorcery, or witchcraft.

In *In the Devil's Snare: The Salem Witchcraft Crisis of 1692*, Mary Beth Norton emphasizes the role the Indian wars of the period played in bringing about the hysteria and persecutions in Salem. "*In the Devil's Snare*," she writes, "...contends that the witchcraft crisis of 1692 can be comprehended only in the context of nearly two decades of armed conflict between English settlers and the New England Indians in both southern and northern portions of the region." Among other things, Norton makes a case for post-traumatic stress disorder (many of the inhabitants of Salem and the surrounding towns were refugees from the devastating Indian wars in Maine) as a factor in the behavior of the "afflicted" young girls who made accusations of witchcraft against others.◊

Beldames and Belles-lettres

By the pricking of my thumbs, something wicked this way comes. — William Shakespeare, Macbeth

∂ Literary Lineage

I've already quoted from Alice Morse Earle's informative 1891 book, *The Sabbath in Puritan New England*. Born in 1853, Earle grew up in Worcester, Massachusetts; besides *The Sabbath* she wrote such books as *Customs and Fashions in Old New England* and *Child Life in Colonial Days*. Drawing upon her extensive knowledge of American history and folklore, she penned an unusual story which appeared in her 1898 collection, *In Old Narragansett* (reprinted in the modern anthology, *Yankee Witches*).

Christmas morning, 1811: Benny Nichols, elderly farmer in the coastal town of Narragansett, Rhode Island, wakes to discover that "the wust snowstorm ye ever see" has blanketed the area. Concerned for the safety of his sheep, he quickly dresses and ventures outside to dig a path through the snow. He finds his flock unharmed, save for one ewe of the rare creeper breed, missing and presumed dead. Weeks later Benny comes upon the ewe trapped in the snow by the side of a hay rick—still alive, having, to stave off starvation, chewed on her own wool.

Benny wraps the poor creature in his cloak and carries it home. His wife, Debby, tenderly nurses it back to health.

Unfortunately it will take months for its fleece to grow back. In the meantime the naked ewe would not long survive the winter cold, so Debby improvises, using material from an old blue coat and red flannel shirt as a makeshift covering. "There was never seen such a comical, stunted, hind-side-foremost caricature."

Despite its outré appearance, the ewe is able to withstand the harsh New England weather and is eventually accepted by the other sheep.

One night the Nicholses receive a visit from a neighbor, gaunt old Tuggie Bannocks, "relic of old slavery times ...who knew how to work powerful charms—traditional relics of Voodooism." Tuggie is nearly out of her mind with fright "'cause I seen the old witch a-ridin'." She has seen the creeper ewe in its homemade garb and mistaken it for her arch rival, old Mum Amey, "a wrinkled half-breed Indian of fabulous age and crabbed temper," who, as a witch, has taken on the shape of a demon.

"'Oh, she was monstrous fearsome to see. Witches don't never go in their own form when they goes to their Sabbaths...She was long an' low like a snake.'"

Benny prepares a mug of flip, her favorite beverage, for the old woman but cannot conceal his mirth. He explains her error. Incensed, and feeling that she is being made fun of, Tuggie refuses to be mollified by further profferings of flip, and pronounces a witch's curse on the farm.

Eventually the curse wears off. But ever after, creeper sheep were known, throughout Narragansett, as "witch-sheep."

"The Witch Sheep" is notable in that, though taking place in the second decade of the nineteenth century, it draws upon many beliefs and superstitions that were carryovers from earlier times. It features not just one, but two practicing witches, Tuggie Bannocks and Mum Amey. Although the author is ambiguous as to whether the former's curse actually worked, she leaves no doubt in the reader's mind that all of the characters fully believed in its efficacy.

The prolific nineteenth-century Massachusetts author, John Greenleaf Whittier, drew upon his extensive knowledge of witch lore to pen a short story, "The Haunted House," which despite its title is not about ghosts, but rather, a witch named Alice Knight, "an ill-tempered and malignant old woman who was seriously suspected of dealing with the Prince of Darkness." Alice's neighbors believe that she casts spells upon them and, in the shape of a black cat, haunts and otherwise bewitches them. Needless to say they greatly fear her. Alice looks the part of the stereotypical witch, too. "She had the long, blue and skinny finger—the elvish locks of gray and straggling hair—the hooked nose, and the long, upturned chin."

The plot revolves around Alice's love for her twenty-five-year-old son, Gilbert, and his love for Mary McOrne, daughter of the wealthy Adam McOrne. Mary loves Gilbert, but refuses to marry the son of a woman known to be a notorious witch. The story does end happily for the young lovers, but only after Alice's machinations fail, and she herself is dead (possibly by her own hand).

Like Earle in "The Witch Sheep," Whittier never commits himself as to whether the witchcraft in his story is real or imagined. "Setting the questions of her powers of witchcraft aside, Alice Knight was actually an evil-hearted woman...When [her neighbors] in the least offended her, she turned upon them with the fierce malison of an enraged Pythoness, and prophesied darkly of some unknown and indescribable evil about to befall them."

A celebrated author who did not hesitate to affirm the authenticity, within the context of the story, of the witchcraft he depicted was Nathaniel Hawthorne, who appropriately enough was born in Salem, Massachusetts—and whose ancestor (with a slight variation in the spelling), John Hathorne, was a judge at the infamous witch trials. Perhaps Hawthorne's best known story involving witches is the frequently anthologized "Young Goodman Brown." The story—which like much of Hawthorne's fiction is highly allegorical (though none the less entertaining)— presents, as real, a witches' sabbat (the devil himself is introduced as a character who attends the nocturnal festivities) and concludes with the spiritual disillusionment of the title character.

A lesser known story by Hawthorne is "Feathertop"—much lighter in tone than "Young Goodman Brown," and more satirical than allegorical. A witch by the name of Mother Rigby (she smokes a pipe which Dickon, an invisible familiar, obligingly lights for her upon command) one day takes it upon herself to make a scarecrow, Feathertop, whom she imbues with life. The plot, such as it is, involves the mild misadventures in self discovery of the hapless scarecrow. According to Yvonne Jocks, editor of *Witches' Brew*, an anthology in which the story is reprinted, "Feathertop" may have served as a model or inspiration for the scarecrow in Frank L. Baum's *Wonderful Wizard of Oz*.◊

On a Clear Day

"Cranberry Madness," no matter how fantastical, is presented as memoir. The two stories that follow, however, are fiction, pure and simple. They were written, and published in literary journals, in the 1980's. I include them here because they illustrate my continued interest in the subject of witchcraft, and because (forgive my immodesty) I think they are fun to read.

The flimsy cotton jacket Bobby wore provided scant protection against the pervading damp. He shivered, brushed the residue of snow from his hair—and wished he could huddle in front of the fire that crackled cheerily in the fireplace across the room.

Pressing his nose against the glass he stared wistfully at the outside world. Miss Rennie was in her garden clipping the dead blossoms off her rose bushes. Old hag, bent double like some rotting stump sticking up out of the ground—so what, that he had trampled on her precious marigolds. So what, that he had called her names. Big deal!

There, limping onto the patio to sun himself and nurse his injured paw, went the primary cause of Bobby's troubles: Pumpkin, Miss Rennie's orange tabby. Mean old cat. Always chasing after birds. Always scratching around in the sand. Even now, Bobby scarcely regretted having thrown the stone.

In the street beyond the picket fence Kevin and Mark passed by on their bikes. They were heading toward the park. Bobby would have waved but his friends were not looking his way and, besides, he knew they would not be able to see him. And so the day dragged on with Bobby, nose flattened against the glass, gazing forlornly at the larger world, wishing he could go outside and play.

In the afternoon Miss Rennie took a nap, then got up to begin supper. After she had set the table, and while the greens from the garden were boiling, she went over to the window to see how her new paper weight was getting on.

Lifting it from the sill, she shook it gently, and watched as the artificial snow drifted through the imprisoned water onto the little boy's head. Poor dear, he looked so cold in that wintry scene. Miss Rennie's mouth cracked wide in a toothless grin. It was the nicest paper weight she had ever made and was sure to amuse her for years and years to come.◊

à Very Important Oate

She had only herself to blame—she had spent too much time hunting for that last item. But *he* was so particular, and she did so want to please him.

Shifting the bundles in her arms, she fumbled her key into the lock and leaned against the door, letting the momentum of her weight carry her into the apartment. Setting the bundles to one side, she took out the pot she used for spaghetti, filled it two-thirds with water, and put it on the stove to boil.

Fur brushed against her bare skin. Absently, she reached down to stroke the cat while setting things straight on the counter. Purring, Montague entwined himself between her ankles.

"Oh, Montague!" she exclaimed, nearly tripping. "Always underfoot! I suppose I'll have to feed you—just when I'm so late. *He*'s coming, you know."

She spooned half a can of Supper Seafood into Montague's plastic dish.

"Phew! Smelly old stuff. How can you be so fond of it?"

Ignoring his mistress, Montague attacked the food greedily.

"There. You're taken care of. Now I can get ready for *him*." She glanced at the kitchen clock. "Oh, only twenty minutes left."

The water was nearly at a boil. She lined everything up on the counter—the exact order for adding the ingredients was important—then went into the pantry for the tin containing the powder. She hurried into the living room where, mumbling, she sprinkled powder from the tin onto the rug. The clock on the mantelpiece read eleven forty-five.

"There's so little time," she murmured, and dashed back into the kitchen. Having consumed two-thirds of his food, Montague sat busily licking his chops, saving the rest for later.

"Yuck, Montague! I should have given you something less odoriferous. Too late now. But I do so want to impress him." She glanced at the stove. "Oh water, *please* boil."

In less than a minute she had her wish. As soon as steam began rising from the pot she began to add the ingredients. With a wooden spoon she normally used for ragout she stirred everything together. Two minutes to twelve she added the final item, the one she had spent so much time looking for. Eye of newt.

The potion ready, she rushed into the living room. There was just enough time to chant the magic spell. As the clock struck midnight mist swirled above the powder, sulfur filled the air, and *he* appeared through a wall of flame.◊

à Witch's Glossary

bell, book, and candle: In the greater excommunication, introduced into the Catholic church in the 8th century, after reading the sentence a bell is rung, a book is closed, and a candle is extinguished. From that moment the excommunicated person is excluded from the sacraments and even from divine worship. The form of excommunication closed with the words "Close the book, quench the candle, ring the bell!" As Dorothy Jacob points out in *Cures and Curses*, "This explains why witches loathed all bells and were afraid of light, especially the lighted candles round a coffin."

broomstick: an actual broomstick or similar implement (such as a magic wand), often made of hazel, astride of which a witch was believed to fly through the air at night. "Before travel, the witches rubbed themselves and their stick with a special Flying Ointment." —*The Encyclopedia of Witchcraft and Demonology*. Such ointments may have consisted of herbs (such as nightshade or monkshood) or other ingredients with hallucinatory properties—or, of a more sinister character, grease rendered from a murdered child or unbaptized baby. For centuries brooms were seen as symbols of feminine power. In ancient Rome, midwives ceremoniously used brooms to sweep the thresholds of a house and drive away evil spirits that might harm mother or child. The broomstick is associated with the hobbyhorse, a stick with an imitation horse's head attached and fashioned into a child's toy, but also believed used by witches to ride about the countryside and fly to their sabbats.

bridle: a harness, sometimes made of human skin, placed by witches over a mount (person or animal). It was commonly believed that a person suffering from disturbed sleep and / or severe body aches had been hagridden (used as a mount by a witch and ridden about the countryside). According to one source, "The placing of a horseshoe near a bedroom was thought effective in eliminating nightmares or hagriding." A local Maine historian reported: "In one of the old houses at Kittery, a part of which was being torn down not long ago, an old witch-bridle was found between the lathing and the outside boarding. It was made of the hair of the tail of a horse, strands of tow, and the inside bark of the yellow birch. A woman who happened to be present knew what it was, and seizing it with the tongs threw it into the fire." Also known as **witch's bridle**. (The latter term, however, was also applied to an implement of torture used to force confessions from persons accused of witchcraft.)

charm: an object, word, phrase, verse, or action used to ward off evil

coven: a group, or cell, of thirteen witches

curse: an utterance or appeal to a deity or other supernatural power for evil to befall a person, animal, object, or other entity

devil's mark (also **devil's seal**): a scar, birthmark, or other blemish believed to have been placed by the devil on the body of a witch who has sworn him allegiance. It "was regarded, when discovered by the examiners, as final and irrefutable evidence of guilt."—Pennethorne Hughes, *Witchcraft*

familiar: an attendant spirit or imp—often in the shape of a cat, toad, hare, owl or other small animal—provided to a witch by the devil, to serve and advise and help perform evil deeds. According to Charles Williams, "The familiar was at once servant and master; it would run about and do mischief but also it would watch and threaten its pretended mistress, whenever that mistress showed signs of failing from her new business." J.A. Brooks tells us that "Satan has to make a formal contract with his witches." In exchange for their soul he gives them a small coin. "The new witch then has a familiar spirit given her, often a black cat, which helps her in her wicked ways and draws her blood for nourishment." Eric Maple defines the "Familiar Spirit" as "An almost exclusively English and Scottish minor Devil, often in animal form."

hagriding: see **bridle**

maleficium: the concept that enchanters existed solely to perform acts of evil and harm (as opposed to the belief that there might also be good or "white" witches). The word derives from Latin, meaning *evil deed*. One ancient book on sorcery states: "Maleficium is a vicious act directed against the body, through the power of the Devil in a tacit or public pact entered into with the witch, through the control of nature, and through the assistance of some person satisfying his own malice, done always, rightly even if obscurely, with the judgment of God permitting." *The Encyclopedia of Witches and Witchcraft* elaborates: "In its narrowest definition, *maleficia* [the plural] meant damage to crops and illness or death to animals. In its broadest, it included anything with a negative impact upon a person: loss of love, storms, insanity, disease, bad luck, financial problems, lice infestations, even death."

philter (also **philtre**): a magic potion

sabbat (also **witches' Sabbath**): an assembly of witches, usually for the purposes of worshipping the devil and engaging in festivities and licentious behavior, such as indiscriminate intercourse, and the indoctrination of new witches

spectral evidence: claims by "victims" to see the specter or shape (invisible to others) of the person bewitching them. Such "evidence" was used in Salem, as elsewhere, to obtain convictions. Eric Maple provides a succinct definition: "The legal fiction that a witch could separate herself from her spirit, which could then, in spectral form, carry out malicious acts on her behalf."

spell: an incantation; words used as a charm; a trance or state of bewitchment

witching hour: midnight, on the night of a full moon

witch's mark: an extra breast or nipple, or any "privy mark" such as a wart, mole, tumor, pile, or other growth or excrescence found on a person's body. Such a mark—believed to be a teat by which a familiar sucked nourishment—was "proof" that the person was a witch. Evidence used against Margaret Jones, the first person executed in Massachusetts for witchcraft, included the following (quoted in *The Witches of Early America* by Sally Smith Booth): "She had (upon search) an apparent teat in her secret parts as fresh as if it had been newly sucked, and after it had been scanned upon a forced search, that was withered and another began on the opposite side."

withershins (also **widdershins**): in a direction contrary to the natural one; in reverse; counterclockwise. *Believed to bring bad luck.* Walking against the sun; walking counterclockwise to cast a spell.

Sources and Books Mentioned in the Text

Along New England Shores by A. Hyatt Verrill (New York: G.P. Putnam's Sons, 1936).

American Gothic ed. by Elizabeth Terry (New York: Barnes & Noble Books, 1997).

The Annotated Mother Goose by Williams S. Baring-Gould and Ceil Baring-Gould (New York: Bramhall House, 1962).

A Book of New England Legends and Folk Lore by Samuel Adams Drake (Boston: Roberts Brothers, 1884).

Cures and Curses by Dorothy Jacob (New York: Taplinger Publishing Company, 1967).

Dighton Rock: A Study of the Written Rocks of New England by Edmund Burke Delabarre (New York: Walter Neale, Publisher of General Literature, 1928).

Dr. LeBaron and His Daughters: A Story of the Old Colony by Jane G. Austin (Boston: Houghton Mifflin Company, 1890; reprinted 1918).

The Encyclopedia of Witchcraft and Demonology by Russell Hope Robbins (New York: Bonanza Books, 1981).

The Encyclopedia of Witches and Witchcraft by Rosemary Ellen Guiley (New York: Facts On File, Inc., 1989).

Folklore in America ed. by Tristram P. Coffin and Hennig Cohen (New York: Double Day & Company, Inc., 1966).

Ghosts and Witches of the Cotswolds by J.A. Brooks (Norwich, England: Jarrold and Sons Ltd., 1986).

A Handbook of New England by Porter E. Sargent (Boston: Sargent's Handbook Series, 1916).

Haunted New England by Mary Bolté (New York: Weathervane Books, 1972).

History of Plymouth, Norfolk and Barnstable Counties by Elroy S. Thompson (New York: Lewis Historical Publishing Company, Inc., 1928).

History of the Town of Carver by Henry S. Griffith (New Bedford: E. Anthony & Sons, Inc., Printers, 1913).

A History of the Town of Freetown (Fall River, Mass.: Press of J.H. Franklin & Company, 1902).

Horse and Buggy Days on Old Cape Cod by Hattie Blossom Fritze (Barnstable, Massachusetts: Great Marshes Press, 1966).

Hunting for Witches by Frances Hill (Beverly Massachusetts: Commonwealth Editions, 2002).

In the Devil's Snare: The Salem Witchcraft Crisis of 1692 by Mary Beth Norton (New York: Alfred A. Knof, 2002).

The Intellectual Life of Colonial New England (second edition) by Samuel Eliot Morison (Ithaca, New York: Cornell University Press, 1956).

An Island Patchwork by Eleanor Early (Boston: Houghton Mifflin Company, 1941).

It's an Old Cape Cod Custom by Edwin Valentine Mitchell (New York: The Vanguard Press, Inc., 1949).

Jonathan Draws the Long Bow by Richard M. Dorson (Cambridge, Massachusetts: Harvard University Press, 1946).

Lands of Sippican by Alice Austin Ryder (printed in New Bedford, Massachusetts, for the Sippican Book Committee, 1934).

Maine Pioneer Settlements: Old York by Herbet M. Sylvester (Boston: W.B. Clarke Co., 1909).

Major Bradford's Town: A History of Kingston 1726-1976 by Doris Johnson Melville (1976).

Massachusetts: Its Historians and Its History by Charles Francis Adams (Boston: Houghton, Mifflin and Company, 1893).

Mattapoisett and Old Rochester by Mary Hall Leonard (1907).

Mooncussers of Cape Cod by Henry C. Kittredge (Boston: Houghton Mifflin Company, 1937).

Mother Goose of Boston (Scotia, New York: *Americana Review*, 1961).

Myths & Legends of Our Own Land (Volumes One and Two) by Charles M. Skinner (Philadelphia: J.B. Lippincott Company, 1896).

The Narrow Land: Folk Chronicles of Old Cape Cod by Elizabeth Reynard, third edition (Boston: Houghton Mifflin Company, 1978).

A Narrative History of the Town of Cohasset by E. Victor Bigelow (Cohasset: 1898).

The Old Coast Road from Boston to Plymouth by Agnes Edwards (Boston and New York: Houghton Mifflin Company, 1920).

The Old Colony Town and the Ambit of Buzzards Bay by William Root Bliss (Boston: Houghton, Mifflin and Company, 1893).

Old Plymouth Trails by Winthrop Packard (Boston: Small, Maynard & Company, 1920).

Old Rochester and Her Daughter Towns by Mary Hall Leonard.

The Pilgrims and Plymouth Colony (New York: American Heritage Publishing Co., Inc., 1961).

The Realm of Ghosts by Eric Maple (London: Pan Books Ltd., 1964).

Rivals of Weird Tales™ ed. by Robert Weinberg, Stefan R. Dziemianowicz, and Martin H. Greenberg (New York: Bonanza Books, 1990).

The Romance of Old New England Rooftrees by Mary C. Crawford (Boston: L.C. Page & Company, 1902).

The Sabbath in Puritan New England by Alice Morse Earle (New York: Charles Scribner's Sons, 1891).

Tall Tales of Cape Cod by Marillis Bittinger (Plymouth, Massachusetts: The Memorial Press, 1948).

The Times of Their Lives: Life, Love, and Death in Plymouth Colony by James Deetz and Patricia Scott Deetz (New York: W.H. Freeman and Company, 2000).

A Treasury of American Superstitions by Claudia de Lys (New York: Philosophical Library, 1948).

A Treasury of New England Folklore (revised edition) ed. by B.A. Botkin (New York: Bonanza Books, 1965).

A Treasury of Witchcraft by Harry E. Wedeck (New York: Philosophical Library, 1961).

What They Say in New England: A Book of Signs, Sayings, and Superstitions collected by Clifton Johnson (Boston. Lee and Shepard Publishers, 1896).

The Whole History of Grandfather's Chair by Nathaniel Hawthorne (Boston: Houghton Mifflin Company, 1896).

Witchcraft by Charles Williams (London: Faber and Faber Limited, 1941).

Witchcraft by Pennethorne Hughes (Baltimore: Penguin Books, 1965).

Witchcraft in Old and New England by George Lyman Kittredge (Cambridge, Massachusetts: Harvard University Press, 1929).

Witches and Witchcraft by the editors of Time-Life Books (Alexandria, Virginia: 1990).

Witches' Brew ed. by Yvonne Jocks (New York: Berkley Books, 2002).

The Witches of Early America by Sally Smith Booth (New York: Hastings House, 1975).

Yankee Witches ed. by Charles G. Waugh, Martin H. Greenberg and Frank D. McSherry, Jr. (Augusta, Maine: Lance Tapley, Publisher, 1988).

The Yankees of Connecticut by W. Storrs Lee (New York: Henry Holt and Company, 1957).